FROM THE INSIDE

MAKING YOUR HOPES, WISHES, AND DREAMS COME TRUE

David D. Dameron

THE PRACTICAL SPIRITUALITY SERIES

authorHOUSE®

AuthorHouse™
1663 Liberty Drive, Suite 200
Bloomington, IN 47403
www.authorhouse.com
Phone: 1-800-839-8640

First published by AuthorHouse 2/6/2008

ISBN: 978-1-4343-5716-8 (sc)
ISBN: 978-1-4343-5715-1 (hc)

Library of Congress Control Number: 2007910306

Printed in the United States of America
Bloomington, Indiana

This book is printed on acid-free paper.

I dedicate this book to my good friends and authors, John and Jan Price. Your work with The Quartus Foundation has inspired me for years, and I appreciate all that you have done to raise the consciousness of those on this planet. This world is a better place because of both of you.

ACKNOWLEDGMENTS

THERE ARE SEVERAL people I would like to thank for assisting me in the publication of this book. My wife, Susan, has become my first editor as she reads the manuscript and offers me suggestions which I have always found to be accurate and insightful.

Denise Stallcup has edited all three of my books, and I deeply appreciate her talent and professionalism as she continues to bring out "my voice" in my writings.

My thanks to Arthur Douët for doing my cover again and offering insights into his visionary art which he shares in this book.

Finally, I would like to thank Jayson Boulet who helped prepare the cover art for the publisher.

"There is no separation between us and God - we are divine expressions of the creative principle. There can be no real lack or scarcity; there is nothing we have to try to achieve or attract: we contain the potential for everything within us."

-- Shakti Gawain

CONTENTS

INTRODUCTION

"There is a power that runs the Universe and the existence of such a power can only be experienced by my personal relationship with this force not someone else's interpretation. This divine knowledge can never be obtained solely by observation, but only by the full participation of my being. I discover inner peace and the love of Spirit through my feeling nature and through direct experience. I do this from the inside."

-- David D. Dameron, 1979

IMAGINE YOU ARE flying in an airplane several miles up in the air, and you are gazing down at a huge iceberg. From your vantage point, the iceberg appears to be gigantic.

But though the iceberg may appear to be massive, that is somewhat of an illusion. As large as it seems, in reality you are seeing only about ten percent of its total size, and it is even more gigantic than it appears. Ninety-percent of the ice mass is under the water.

Life is much the same way - when we live on the surface of life, we are under the illusion that we are experiencing all there is to life. We become immersed in our day-to-day routines of showering, eating, and doing chores. We drive to work or to other destinations, watch television, play golf, or engage in a hobby. We deal with our relationships, go to the doctor, pay bills, and think about retiring someday.

All of these things are important to maintaining the quality of life we desire; but there is another level to life - one that is occurring beneath the surface. For it is in the depths of our consciousness, our thoughts, our emotions, our beliefs, and our connection with our spirit that the true meaning and possibilities for our lives emerge.

What lies beneath the surface is mysterious, fascinating and powerful. Consider a simple seed – each spring, I plant beans, and working in my garden one day I realized the seed I held in my hand contained enormous potential. Inside the seed I held was the blueprint for what it could become - a bean plant. It required only an environment supportive of its potential – water and sunlight – to transform into a beautiful and prolific bean plant. That was its destiny.

So are your thoughts, and mine, very much like that seed – what is planted, grows. If I plant a seed of compassion and caring in the way I teach and work with people, what might I receive in return? If I choose to harm someone or commit a crime, what would I receive in return? Life continually reflects our thoughts and our actions back to us.

This book is based on the understanding that *how we live our lives (the seeds we plant) and the quality of our lives are intimately connected to the nature of our thoughts, feelings, and emotions – to what is going on inside of us.* If you have something going on in your life that is causing you pain and discomfort, then you must be willing to look beneath the surface at your thoughts, your feelings, and your actions. The source of what you struggle with lies, not in the world outside yourself, but within yourself.

Let me give you an example from my own life. In applying this understanding that what I experience comes from within me, I realized one day why I had always had so much conflict with many of my bosses. I never wanted to take their directions and listen to them. I realized that my reactions to my bosses were representative of my relationship with my father. When I was young, I rebelled against my father for trying to direct my life. Once I healed my relationship with my father, my relationship with my boss improved dramatically, and I've had much better relationships with supervisors since then. My relationships with my bosses were only playing out what I had not resolved with my father. Once those unresolved issues were addressed, my problems with bosses cleared up.

Let me give you another example of how this external and internal process manifested in my own life. Being self-employed, I used to believe that the financial health of my business was dependant on other people. I believed I could only be successful if others returned my telephone calls, allowed me to meet with them, and wanted to do business with me.

When my business was experiencing a low income cycle I would become very impatient with potential clients if they did not return my telephone calls. I told myself my business was suffering because clients showed me no courtesy or respect. But I also noticed that, when I was doing well financially, clients were much more likely to return my calls.

What I realized was that my impatience during low income periods was not caused by clients' behavior, but by my own insecurity about my financial stability. I feared for my future if the business failed to pick up. My attitude – fear of failure – was sending out a negative message, and that was the reason my potential clients were not calling me back. They were merely reflecting back to me my own insecurities, just as my bosses had reflected back to me my unresolved relationship with my father.

Recognizing this dynamic, I've worked to let go of my anxieties and focus my attention on what is positive and possible. Now my relationships are strong and positive, people return my calls, and my business is prosperous. What I send out – confidence, faith in abundance, and belief in my own success – returns to me, time and again.

FROM THE INSIDE was written to help you understand that *everything* that is occurring in your external world is merely a reflection of what is occurring inside you. The quality of your relationships, your career, your financial situation, and your health is directly related to the quality of your thoughts, feelings, beliefs, and emotions.

My contention in this book is the same as that of my previous two books, REMEMBERING OUR SPIRIT and SEEING THE SACRED IN LIFE. I hold that we are divine beings - co-creators, so to speak - and the purpose of our lives is to bring forth our divinity through the power of our choice-making. To show you how to make your hopes, wishes, and dreams come true, this book will take you to the source of all good things in your life. From this sacred place, you can consider your own life from a spiritual perspective, and understand that your spirit is the source of your own abundance.

A wise lady once told me that I saw the "fruit of life," but I was not seeing the "vine." What she was trying to point out to me was that I recognized abundance in my life, but I needed to realize and appreciate the *source* of that abundance, which was God or Spirit. Looking only on the surface, I saw my clients as the source of my prosperity. Looking beneath the surface, I saw it was Spirit that was the true source of my abundance.

Seeing your life from a place of Spirit will show you that everything that manifests in your life begins inside you. Everything in your life has come from the Source. Everything!

The ramifications of this dynamic are astounding, not just in our own lives but globally. Poverty need not exist. We can keep many potential health challenges at bay, and better manage those we do face. Everyone who desires a perfect relationship can find that relationship. The perfect job, and financial independence, is available to everyone. There do not have to be wars. These are the positive possibilities – but keep in mind, *all* possibilities exist in Spirit, both the positive and the negative. What we choose to experience is just that - a *choice*. If you want to change what manifests in your life, change you perceptions, and bring faith and a positive approach to your attentions, your thoughts and your actions.

Remember: *all conditions in your life are created by your mind.* This is truly the grand secret of the universe. Quantum Physicists have determined that the physical world is a reflection of how we look at things, and that by observing matter we change it. Atomic particles, which are what matter is composed of, respond to our thoughts!

We have been taught that the physical universe is more real – more solid – than our own thoughts, and that we are at the mercy of circumstance. It is true that our problems feel real. Financial and health challenges feel real. War seems to be the only way to resolve conflict. Many situations in our lives and our world appear rigid and unchangeable. We work hard each day and sometimes wonder why we are not making better progress. The intent of this book – its purpose - is to suggest to you that you try a different approach to your life. To suggest that maybe life is not something that *happens* to us, but rather something we are creating through our thoughts and perceptions.

Is it truly possible that by changing your thoughts and our perceptions, you can make significant changes in your life? The answer to this is an emphatic *yes*! By practicing the guidelines given to you in this book, you become your own scientist in this experiment, and the laboratory of your life is the proof. If you believe that you deserve only the best in life, then you must "think" and "act" as if everything you desire is already at hand. And here's the good news: it is!

Just remember the example of the bean plant. The innate potential of the bean plant is locked in the seed. In other words, the *blueprint* of the perfect bean plant is locked within the seed.

What blueprint, what potential, do you think is locked inside each of us? What do you think is possible for your own life? What idea or image is unfolding as we live our lives?

My contention is that, at our essence, we are divine beings. Ultimately, we cannot express anything but divinity because that is what our blueprint is, much like the blueprint of the bean seed. But most people I see every day continue to deny their own divinity through poor choice making, and that creates overwhelming challenges. Changing that dynamic is just a matter of becoming aware of our choices, and aware of who and what we truly are.

THE FORMAT OF this book is much like that of my other two books. Each chapter begins with a story to illustrate the subject matter. Each story is followed by short passages that help you reflect on the material and journal your thoughts.

The book outlines four steps that are the key to creating *anything* you want in your life. Each step is presented at various points in the book prior the chapters. The stages that are the keys to the life you want are:

#1 Invite the Idea

#2 Feel the Feeling

#3 Design the Blueprint

#4 Participate in the Outcome

I SUGGEST YOU read the entire book first, and then return to the first chapter, read a passage each day, and write down your reflections. There is also a sample goal sheet in the Appendix of the book. This goal sheet will guide you in writing down a goal you'd like to achieve and taking the steps necessary for you to manifest that goal.

Don't be concerned if you haven't read my first two books; each of my books stands alone. It is not at all necessary for you to have read the previous books to reap all the benefits of this one.

This volume does differ from the previous two in that it contains a powerful feature they did not have. After the introduction to each chapter, and following the action step that is included with each chapter, you will find an affirmation for you to use. Affirmations are powerful tools that verbalize your intention, and crystallize the idea that the book has led you to create in your imagination. When each affirmation is presented to you, just take a few moments to speak its words with great passion and feeling. Doing so will give a tremendous boost to attracting the very thing you desire!

My final reminder to you is this: if you wish to create more joy in your life and realize all of your hopes, wishes, and dreams, then you must be willing to look beneath the surface and inside yourself. You must begin to understand that your world is a reflection of your thoughts, words, and actions.

If you are willing to take responsibility for what occurs in your world, and if you have the courage to find your spirit and *think in terms of your spirit,* then anything you desire and any hopes that you have for this world will come to you.

I hope that you will enjoy the journey you are about to embark upon, and I commend you for choosing to read this book. I am excited for you, for the possibilities you will realize, and for the wonderful changes you will make in your own life!

STAGE ONE

Invite the Idea

"We do not look at the things which are seen as being eternal. Behind the visible and changeable is the changeless reality, the Eternal One, working in time and space for the expression of Itself. The Divine Ideas stand back of all human thought, seeking admittance through the doorway of the mind."

-- Ernest Holmes
from THE SCIENCE
OF THE MIND

IDEA

(n., thought, concept, design, insight, theory, belief, undertaking, brainstorm, inspiration)

HAVE YOU EVER considered that all creation - everything that exists - began with an idea? The chair you sit in, the car you drive, the house you live in, the stars in the sky, your very existence – all were originally ideas.

So where do ideas come from? What is the source of an idea? On the surface, it would appear that ideas are first conceived in the imagination. Some theories suggest they originate in the subconscious mind.

These theories don't have physical proof to establish them as fact. If you opened the skull to examine the brain and a brain cell, you would not find an idea. So if we can assume, for a moment, that ideas do not originate in the brain, then where might ideas come from?

As with most philosophical questions, there are a wide variety of theories and approaches that address the question. A number of philosophers have suggested that innate ideas are not derived from experience. Plato believed that ideas were immaterial objects existing outside of the mind. Later, Greek and medieval philosophical theories held that ideas originated in the mind of God. To German philosopher, Georg Wilhelm Friedrich, ideas were representative of the overall pattern or purpose of the universe.

For the purposes of this book, I would ask you to consider that there is a *source* behind all ideas, a place where all ideas *originally* come from – and that you are and have always been connected to this source. The source behind all ideas is the divine - a power that is all-knowing, all-powerful, and everywhere present.

In *Stage One* – the first of four stages discussed in this book that will help you achieve the life you want - we will be exploring the power of an idea. In order to create the life that you desire, you need to begin with an idea. From the conception of the idea, you must then envision your idea clearly in your imagination, and associate it with strong feelings. This book will guide you in approaching your ideas in this way so you can reap the substantial benefits they can bring to you.

But there is one other thing to be aware of as you work with your idea. Remember that you are a divine being, a co-creator working hand-in-hand with the power that permeates the entire universe. Just think about that. *You* are intimately connected to the very power that – with your assistance - creates everything you see and experience in the physical universe. I mentioned "with your assistance" because the creative power cannot manifest your ideas without your input as well - if you do not act on an idea, it does not happen!

Therefore, whatever you hope for, wish for, and dream of is available at any moment. You just need to learn how to put your ideas into action. Whatever challenge you attract or whatever opportunity you create - you are not acting alone. You are part of a miraculous process that unfolds as you embrace and act on an idea.

Knowing where ideas come from and being cognizant that nothing is withheld from you, I hope you feel a sense of excitement at the wealth of possibilities that are available to you. Knowing that your external world is a reflection of your focus and what is occurring inside of you puts you in a position of creating a world filled with infinite possibilities.

How do you tap into this infinite source of power and ideas? What is possible in your life when you do so? Welcome to *Stage One*.

ACTION STEP

To GET YOU started on your journey, listed below are several *Life Impact Areas*. On a piece of paper, describe what your "ideal life" would look like in each of these areas, where applicable. Don't hold back – give this exercise the time and attention necessary to fully express yourself.

Life Impact Areas

Spiritual:

Personal:

Financial:

Career:

Family/ Relationship:

Social/ Emotional:

Physical/ Health:

Mental/ Educational:

AFTER YOU HAVE written down the description of your ideal life (your hopes, wishes, and dreams) for each of these areas where applicable, list some concrete steps you could take to bring your ideal life into fruition in each of these areas. For example, if you wanted to lose weight and improve your health in the physical/ health area, you might write down walking or exercise as a practical step.

If you are unsure of what steps you could take to help you realize your ideal life, just continue reading this book plan to and come back to this area. Continue to work on your list until all the aspects of your ideal life are fully realized. In addition to outlining your ideal life, you will be referring back to this list with other exercises in this book.

You might also practice meditation on the areas you are unsure of, asking Spirit to show you what you should do. Sit quietly in a chair and close your eyes, and ask, with feeling, that you be shown how to determine your ideal life. Then watch for Spirit's response – it may come in unexpected ways, through something you read in a magazine or something you see on a television show. Pay attention to *everything*, including what people say to you. Use your close friends as resources as well, telling them what you are trying to accomplish. Practice this meditation each day, sitting quietly and listening to your real inner voice, which is talking to you amid all the other voices in your head. Journal the impressions you are receiving, no matter how odd the impressions are.

Remember that *nothing* is withheld from you. You do not have to force anything. You just need to **invite the idea** by asking Spirit to show you what to do next. And all of this process begins and takes place inside of you. You are connected to the source that created the entire universe, and the Source *always* responds to your invitation. Now you can begin to understand the famous biblical quote; "Ask and you shall receive". This is a law of nature. Your spirit awaits your command!

CHAPTER ONE

Soul

"A god within each human breast."

-- Ovid

SOUL

(n. spirit, mind, warmth of emotion, feeling, essence, heart, center, being)

A FRIEND SENT me a wonderful story years ago. Though I have never been able to identify the author, it's a story that I have heard many times since, and one I thought you would enjoy.

One day an expert on the subject of time management was speaking to a group of business students and to drive home a point, he used an illustration that his students would never forget.

As this man stood in front of the group of high-powered over-achievers, he said, "Okay, time for a quiz." Then he pulled out a one-gallon, wide-mouthed mason jar and set it on a table in front of him. He produced a dozen fist-sized rocks and carefully placed them, one at a time, into the jar. When the rocks reached the top of the jar and no more rocks would fit inside, he asked his students, "So what do you think? Is this jar full?"

Everyone in the class answered, "Yes." Then the presenter said, "Really?" He reached under the table and pulled out a bucket of gravel, dumped some gravel in and the jar and shook it, causing pieces of gravel to work themselves down into the spaces between the big rocks. Then he smiled and asked the group once more, "How about now? Is the jar now full?"

By this time the class was onto him. "Probably not," one of the students answered. "Good!" the instructor replied. He again reached under the table and brought out a bucket of sand. He started dumping the sand into the jar, and it went into all the spaces left between the rocks and the gravel. Once again he asked the question, "Is this jar full?"

"No!" the class shouted. Once again the instructor said, "Good!" Then he grabbed a pitcher of water and began to pour it until the jar was filled to the brim. Then he looked up at the class and asked, "What is the point to this exercise?" One eager beaver raised his hand and said, "The point is, no matter how full your schedule is, if you try really hard, you can always fit some more things in to it!"

"No," the speaker replied gently, "That's not the point. This exercise teaches us that you must put the big rocks in first, or you'll never fit them in at all."

———————————

MY INTENT IN sharing this story with you is to urge you to think about what the "big rocks" are in your life - then put those into your jar first! What goal do you have that takes priority over every other element of your life? How about a project you want to finish? Time with your loved ones? Your faith, your education, your finances? Teaching and mentoring others? If you don't put your big rocks in first, you will never get them in at all.

Most goal-setting techniques concentrate on the end result - winning the race, losing weight, saving money for a trip. It is important to keep the end result in mind, but perhaps the biggest rock you should consider is the source of your abundance.

You see, I believe that we take many essential things for granted - the air we breathe, the food on our table, the job we have, our health. Did you ever stop to think what is behind all that is provided for us? What intelligence created this perfect environment we live in?

The same intelligence that created our environment helps us reach the goals we set. Why in our darkest hours does the very thing we desire appear? You are a soul, and that means you have choice and, through the power of choice, you get to choose what you want.

You have the opportunity to *choose* to live a fulfilling life - or you can choose the opposite. In either case, the thoughts you think, the words you speak, and the actions you take all lead to attracting the very thing you are putting your focus on, whether that focus is positive or negative.

As a soul, you are connected to the very power that created this universe. This power does not make judgments about what you should or should not have. It only expresses itself according to whatever ideas are impressed upon it.

Knowing the connection between power and thoughts does not explain away the mystery of existence. I still cannot always understand why "bad things" happen to apparently good people. I cannot begin to fathom why a child dies or an airplane crashes.

What I can say is that my "big rock" each and every day is expressing gratitude to God. I try to listen for this power's guidance in every moment, and that can be challenging at times. But when I desire something, I make it a point to hold nothing back in my expression of what it is I desire.

Sometimes, when I forget who I am, I become entangled in some less-than-positive situation I have attracted to myself. Many times, in my low rhythms, I forget to turn to my source for strength and energy. But as soon as I do, the dark clouds part, a brilliant light returns to my heart, and everything in my life improves immediately.

Because this process takes place first from *inside* of me, I always begin by going inside. I ask for guidance. I envision the idea for something I desire. I let myself truly feel it, and if I desire it, I act on bringing it into my life. I am a soul, and I am creating my world. I can choose to create this world from my divinity – which only conceives of the positive - or I can create it from my personality, which sees good and bad, abundance and lack, love and fear.

In reality, there is no lack. There is no fear. There is only *Source*, and when I put that big rock into my jar first, then all else in my life takes on a different perspective. Always remember the power of your choice-making, your thoughts, your words, and your actions. Remember you, in reality, are a divine being - so choose wisely!

ACTION STEP

GO BACK TO your list of possible **Life Impact Areas** that you wrote down in *Stage One*. Considering them from the perspective that you are a divine being and a soul – a being who can choose - look at the ideas you have generated. Do they represent what you *really* want? Are they ideas that truly mean something to you, or are they ideas someone has imposed upon you? Would you risk anything and everything you have to make them happen? As you read this book, keep working with your list of Life Impact Areas, and as you form new ideas, keep refining your list until it is truly representative of what you want in your life.

AFFIRMATION

Everything in my life is in divine right order, and I now recognize, accept, and follow the divine plan of my life as it reveals itself to me.

QUANTUM PHYSICS IS a branch of science that is concerned with the relationship between matter and energy at the subatomic level. What quantum physicists are discovering is that matter is influenced by the way we look at things. What does their discovery mean to you?

This discovery is important because matter (which is made up of particles) responds, or is formed, according to the way we look at something – according to our thoughts. It means that ideas influence matter. When we envision an idea, the particles of the universe start to bring it into physical form. Carried to its logical conclusion, one could say that, in each moment, we choose what we want to experience according to our thoughts.

Quantum physics teaches us about possibilities, in that we live in a Universe, which has formed according to thoughts. Take a moment to imagine the impact of this reality. Can you begin to envision the impact this reality has on your life, the possibilities it poses? *Nothing* is withheld from you. As a soul, you get to choose and life brings what you choose to you! What do you want in life?

My Thoughts —

"Everyone one of us has in himself a continent of undiscovered character. Happy is one who acts the Columbus to his own soul."

-- Sir J. Stevens

As a soul, I have chosen in my lifetime to do what I can to help people improve the quality of their lives. Many times I have wondered whether, as a person and as a professional, I have truly been successful in helping people.

Then one day I received the following note from a client who reminded me that no effort goes unnoticed in life. I had given her a book as a gift. She wrote, "I can truthfully say that this book is one of the best gifts I have ever received. Yet, how can I say this when I have read only two pages of it? I can say this because every word so far rings so true to my spirit, my core sense of knowing. It is as if someone has finally put into words what I have felt for so long. You, Mr. Dameron, are the one I say thank you to, from the bottom of my heart."

It is in these moments that I realize that I am making a difference in people's lives because I choose to make a difference! In whose life have you made a difference?

My Thoughts —

"Choose thy love. Love thy choice."

-- German Proverb

THE CHOICES WE make create "ripples" in our lives. When you choose to do a kind act for someone or assist an individual in need, your act can inspire that person to *choose* to have a positive effect in someone else's life. I was reminded of this today when I received a call from a client of mine who is an Associate Superintendent of a school system. This person told me that a couple of principals had remarked how much my workshops had changed their lives. The impact went beyond their professional lives – they said their families were communicating better at home, and that everyone was practicing better self-care (an area my workshops urge people to focus on).

While I was glad to receive this telephone call for its own sake, it also reminded me of ripples. I had an impact on the parents of the family, yet the impact I made extended beyond them. As a soul, I am becoming aware of how my words and actions can have such profound effects. In whose life have you been responsible for such "ripples"?

My Thoughts —

"Here's a test to find whether your mission on earth is finished: if you're alive, it isn't."

-- Richard Bach

I OFTEN GET ideas from a variety of sources - books, magazines, newspapers, television shows, movies, talk radio, billboards, other people, and songs, to name a few. And like you, there are times that ideas just seem to spring from my mind. The source of the idea doesn't matter; when you desire something or you have a need, just ask your spirit that you be shown what to do and then just pay attention to everything, because Spirit doesn't always answer us in ways we expect.

For example, I was struggling with the title to my second book – every title I came up with was already assigned to a book in print. I finally asked Spirit to show me what the title should be. Soon after, I was listening to a talk show and the person being interviewed said that our lives would be better if we just would see the sacred in life in all of our affairs. I realized in that moment that the title to my second book would be *Seeing the Sacred in Life*.

Life responds to our requests. Just remember to ask, and be patient and attentive until your request is answered.

My Thoughts —

"The idea does not belong to the soul; it is the soul that belongs to the idea."

-- Charles Sanders Pierce

I had lunch today with a good friend, and I was expressing how challenging it was to work with my clients on conceptual topics such as of the power of our thoughts, the work of quantum physicists, and where ideas possibly come from. I told her that people who look at the physical world through the intellect see things differently than those who see the world through their intuition.

I believe it is necessary to trust your intuition in order to understand my books, and to understand Spirit, as I use the term. Those with an intellectual viewpoint want me to prove things to them scientifically. Ultimately, I believe that to truly understand the purpose of life and to comprehend the power of our thoughts and ideas, we have to learn to tap into our intuitive abilities. I believe everyone has intuitive ability - intuition is rooted in experience and direct contact with our spirits. Intuition emanates from the inside! Can you think of how your intuition has served you in the past?

My Thoughts —

"One thing that never ceases to amaze me...is the growth of understanding."

-- Alice Walker

OFTEN, AS PART of the workshops I conduct, I ask my clients to reflect on whether their attitudes and their choices impact the quality of their world. I tell them that the quality of their lives is directly related to the quality of their relationship with their spirit. When I asked a class one day what I meant by their "spirit," I was amazed at how many people do not have a concept of spirit do not know what their spirit feels like or even have an idea of what their spirit is.

That people have no concept of spirit at all is indicative of how caught up we are in our day-to-day lives. I realized my clients never or seldom considered that there was more going on in life than what their eyes could see. As a soul, I am in charge of how my internal and external worlds are working. I frequently tell my clients to "slow down!" I need to do the same, so I can reflect on what is behind everything that I see happening in my world. I need to make time to reflect and meditate on how my spirit feels and how my spirit talks to me. I then need to carry that connection into my daily affairs. How could you strengthen your connection with your spirit?

My Thoughts —

"You never find yourself until you face the truth."

-- Pearl Bailey

19

Wʜᴇɴ I ᴀᴍ pondering a question or a situation, it always amazes me when the answer, or insight, shows up unexpectedly. I was traveling to a conference recently to promote my second book, and while sitting in the airport, I was composing a speech I was going to deliver in the near future. I was thinking about the words "human potential," and considering that we all have so much untapped potential. I was connecting this idea to the thousands of people I have trained and how I have been touched by so many of their personal stories, each filled with joy and tragedy. As my airplane was called and I started walking down the ramp to the plane, I saw a poster on the wall advertising the airline on which I was traveling. Written on the poster was, "Every passenger has a story."

This slogan was exactly the illustration I had needed for my speech. It's true – we do all have great stories, and we are all passengers traveling together in life. I was grateful to spirit in this moment, and the poster was a nice reminder that life and spirit are talking to me all of the time. I just need to pay attention!

My Thoughts —

"For the unlearned, old age is winter; for the learned, it is the season of the harvest."

-- Hasidic Proverb

WHEN I WAS a child attending Sunday school, I was taught the concept of heaven and hell, and told that hell was a place where lost souls go and suffer. In my experience, religion also looks at heaven as being some place in the sky where a soul goes if the person has lived life in a certain way.

I just do not believe in that approach any more. I believe that as a soul, I create my own heaven and hell through my choice making. I know some people who believe they are in hell right now, and they are alive! As souls, we gain experience in our choice making; when we make choices from our true spirit, then we are in heaven.

What happens to the soul after it dies is open to many interpretations - but if I am creating my reality through my thoughts and beliefs, I choose to believe that heaven is here, now. After I die, my soul will continue according to the experiences I have had and the lessons I've learned while in a physical body. This reminds me of a saying I've heard, "Life is not a dress rehearsal!"

My Thoughts —

"Ideals are like stars; you will not succeed
in touching them with your hands....you
choose them as your guides, and following
them, you will reach your destiny."

-- Carl Schurz

I LEARNED A great technique today to address some of the issues and challenges in my life. As a soul, I have made many choices in my lifetime, and some of those choices have created pain and unhappiness in my life. I made those choices as best I could, from the place I was in consciousness at that time. As I grew older (and, hopefully, wiser) my choice making improved, though poor choices made in my past do, at times, still haunt me.

So I learned to take advantage of a technique called "rewriting my past." This approach involved taking a piece of paper and rewriting some of the events in my life in which I had made poor choices. I rewrote the event in terms of how I *should* have handled the situation – and in doing so, I found that I began to let go of the bad memories of these events. I cleared up issues with my parents, with some of my friends and with clients. I found this exercise very healthy for my soul. What events would you like to rewrite in your life?

My Thoughts —

"The willingness to accept responsibility for one's own life is the source from which self-respect springs."

-- Joan Didion

TODAY I HEARD an interview with Peter Russell, the author and quantum physicist. Russell talked about his belief that everything we see and experience is a projection that begins in our minds. He said that we must begin to realize and to understand that there is literally *nothing* outside of ourselves – that there is only consciousness or perception and that, in terms of "matter," we really do not know what is out there.

Listening to Russell, I realized how important it is for me to find my authentic self, the part of me that is spirit, and that sees the world through the eyes of my spirit. My authentic self is the part of me that treats myself as if I were spirit, and treats everyone around me as if they are spirit as well. The reality is that we *are* all spirit; when the day comes that we realize this fact, then we will witness and experience heaven on earth.

My Thoughts —

*"I want to say in the last four seconds of
my life that I tried to do my best."*

-- Ruben Blades

CHAPTER TWO

IMAGINATION

"Thought, like the seed, germinates and comes forth, like the tree, in the form of an idea. It then waits like the fruit to be eaten."

-- Phineas P. Qimby

IMAGINATION
(n. mind's eye, mental imagery, visualization, dream world, fancy, creativity, inventiveness)

I HAVE ALWAYS been drawn to individuals who display a high degree of imagination. Historically, I've been interested in Einstein, da Vinci, Michaelangelo, Picasso, Mozart, and Edison to name a few – and in my personal life, there have been a number of individuals who have inspired me with their imaginations. One of those individuals is Arthur Douët, who has always inspired me with his artistic ability. Arthur does all of the artwork for the covers of my books.

Arthur studied at Ecole des Beaux-Arts in Paris between 1966 and 1969 as well as at the Art Students League in New York in 1974, and calls himself a "visual artist." He has shown his artwork in galleries and at conventions in France, the United States, including Hawaii, and also in Bali, Indonesia and Jamaica, W.I.

Apart from his mystical symbolic art and portraits, on invitation, he teaches a creative expression art course on "Your Power to Create" throughout the United States. I recently asked Arthur to describe the process he goes through when he paints and how the imaginative process is engaged when he does so. Arthur sent me a letter responding to my request; I've decided not to edit the letter and allow you, the reader, to hear first-hand how this imaginative and talented soul expresses his art. His letter began with this heading:

THE GROUND OF A RELAXED MIND: A FERTILE BASE

"THE EMERGENCE OF a creative solution in the arena of design seems to be forever a mystery to me. It does not follow a pattern of reason or logic. Rather, it seems to defy that law. To arrive at a creative outcome calls for entering the silence of allowing the mind to go blank or even wander aimlessly. Silence, wherein thinking is abandoned, remains the genesis of creative wisdom.

My advice to students of art is 'be not afraid of the blank mind. It is no waste of time.' Like the oyster that creates a new priceless pearl or the musician composing music, or the poet of a poem, the artist honors listening *outside* the box of reason. I teach my students to let go of mental control by closing their eyes, allowing their hands to make brush movements at random across the surface of their paper. When they open their eyes they can see the work of the unconscious at play. Then with the interplay of the right and left hemispheres, they can 'join the dots' into composition."

THE POWER OF FOCUS

"What of pre-determination?" The mind can preface the process by ascending to the spiritual realm of Being and asking for guidance. This is all-important for me. I combine deep breathing with meditation or contemplation to be inspired."

THE BAROMETER OF FEELINGS

"The feminine nature (expressing through the brain's right hemisphere) comes into play when we let go and trust our feelings as we focus on emerging images that appear on the screen of the mind. The good feelings of 'yes' are often mild ones and those of 'no' are more in keeping with logical deductions, although they shout at times."

COLORS AND SYMBOLS
OF GREAT IMPORT

"The creator is wise to pay attention to colors and symbols that both indicate metaphorical meanings and values. In my experience, the color blue signifies a sacred energy of dedication and loyalty to one's highest *ideal*. Yellow speaks of joy and expansion in its embrace of life. Radiant and transparent red is also sacred, representing the divine power that lifts us. Green shows up for integration with all creation, rest and healing. Orange signifies courage and determination of one's sense of integrity and self-respect. Violet overtones lend their energies to the transformation and transmutation of our basic mental and emotional nature in transition. Violet, indigo, gold and silver are colors that vibrate refinement in the development of soul awareness or God-consciousness."

ASPECT OF FAITH

"Faith is important as a component in the creative process as practiced by one who chooses to be an aspirant of spiritual realization. Faith comes alive in me when the mind is stilled in contemplative openness to receive in the now moment. This condition leads to knowing or oneness with the Divine. It is facilitated with the practice of breath movement, toning and visualizing the final outcomes desired even without details or specifics.

I find it important to let go of the sense of urgency of the 'when and wherefore' of the result. When the image does not manifest in keeping with the mind's expectations, that's the time to release it, sleep on it, so as to awaken with a clearer sense the following day.

When I was searching for a design for David's second book, SEEING THE SACRED IN LIFE, I sensed the focus of centrality was the Divine 'in whom we live and move our being' as the ever-present constant 'whose center is everywhere.' This was the real force bringing the male and female into a blessed union 'made in heaven.' Both of these light beings were lit up by the same divine fire emanating from them. When I breathed into this drawing, I knew that it was blessed by the Inner Light."

THE BELOVED GODDESSES

"Waiting in quiet receptivity - I am.
I listen to the music of the spheres
And attune to the Moon.
Deep in indigo night of Mother's womb
I know I AM at this moment of NOW
--a child of the Universe!
I ascend to the Everlasting arms
In the stillness of the evening
I hear the angels sing
Come join your sister goddesses
In their triumphant ascension
Into the Light they have always been."

-- Arthur Douët

THE POWER OF imagination is such a wonderful mystery. Arthur Douët is someone who shows us its possibilities because of his ability to tap into that unlimited source of ideas. I recently listened to a promotional piece for a series on the Science Fiction channel, and the speaker began talking about the power of imagination.

Some of his remarks about imagination included, "Imagination is your inner voice or the center of everything . . . Exploring the mysteries of life guarded by a key — our imagination . . .See the invisible, explore the possibility . . .It transports you to other worlds or it gives you the power to transform your world."

As a soul, you are learning how to create the world of your desires through the power of your choice-making. In doing so, you develop your consciousness or your awareness. So everything that happens to you occurs first in your consciousness. It is through your imagination that the invisible - the word of ideas - takes shape.

Therefore, everything you see in the world has been an idea that has taken shape because it was first conceived in your imagination. The important thing for you to realize is that *the power of your imagination is really about possibility*. If you can see something you desire in your mind's eye and if you believe that what you desire is possible, then the universe goes to work to bring that desire into manifestation for you.

Nothing is withheld from you, and you are limited only by your thinking and your belief patterns. Take time to contemplate what I am saying to you. The imagination process is like a direct connection with your divinity, and this connection allows you to create whatever you desire in your life.

ACTION STEP

LOOK AT YOUR list of possible **Life Impact Areas** that you wrote down in *Stage One*. Choose the area you'd like to concentrate on first. In a quiet setting, sit with your eyes closed and envision in detail the very thing that you desire. Feel it. See how you feel as you participate in the manifestation of your desire. Celebrate in the joy of your accomplishment. This exercise will be like watching a movie, but I want you to go one step further and imagine yourself *in* the movie. The power of this action step will become clear as you continue reading this book.

AFFIRMATION

*Each day I practice using my imagination,
and I now understand the divine wisdom
and guidance that is directing my life in
each moment.*

IMAGINATION IS THE key that opens the flow from your spirit. Our brains and our hearts act as antenna - as we are constantly sending thoughts out, we are also receiving thoughts and messages. Have you ever wondered what the source of these internal messages is? Have you ever considered the power of your imagination and how being focused on what you desire brings into creation the very thing you are envisioning? If everything that we see and experience is created by our minds, then what miracles are possible in our lives, through the power of imagination? The key point to reflect on is that manifesting your ideas and bringing things into physical reality all starts inside of you.

My Thoughts —

"Imagination is the eye of the soul."

-- Joseph Joubert

IF YOU ARE struggling to understand that everything we see and all ideas happen inside of ourselves first, consider this example. In our brains, with our eyes open we can look at an object like a chair. With our eyes closed, we can still see that same chair. So what is reality? Is what we are seeing happening outside of us or inside of us? Have you ever had the feeling of observing yourself performing some kind of activity? If you are observing yourself, then who is the observer – and who is being watched? If you opened up your brain, you would not find an observer. These questions suggest we can have different realities depending upon the *way* we look at things. Therefore, it would make sense to look at things from a positive viewpoint so that the quality of your outer world would be a reflection of those thoughts. Now imagine how your world would look if you saw it through the eyes of your spirit and your divinity. Can you imagine such a world?

My Thoughts —

"Tickle your mind."

-- Lindsey Collier

I HAVE NEVER been that attracted to really sweet foods, but I now understand why people eat chocolate. The other night, my wife wanted me to try some high-grade chocolate. After resisting, I ate a couple of pieces. A few minutes later I realized I felt very energized, and I found myself thinking about possibilities for new books and new creative projects. I could not go to sleep at my normal time. I felt fantastic. When I tried some chocolate a couple of nights later, to my wife's delight, I experienced the same response. After doing some research on chocolate, I found that high-grade chocolate actually triggers positive chemicals in our brains, which explains why I was feeling so creative. I laughed at myself when I told my wife that if I kept this up, I would be a five hundred pound person with a great imagination. To be honest, I'd prefer to create these heightened states in a natural way - but in either case, I like how it feels when I feel connected to my spirit and I can play with my imagination.

My Thoughts —

"The source and center of all man's creative power…is his power of making images, or the power of imagination."

-- Robert Collier

WHEN I FEEL sluggish or uninspired about my life, I realize I simply need to get more creative. Anytime I begin writing a new book or when I am designing a new workshop, I notice how my moods tend to stabilize and I become more energized. Staying creative and not allowing myself to fall into some of my lethargic patterns is how I stay in contact with my spirit. Whether I am working in the yard, engaging in a hobby, or playing the piano, I realize these activities affect my emotional state in a positive way. I feel better about myself when I am productive and creative. We are all creative, and our creativity stimulates our imaginations. What activities can you engage in that make you feel connected to your spirit?

My Thoughts —

"Too low they build, who build beneath the stars."

-- Malcolm S. Forbes

ONE OF THE joys of my training and consulting practice is that it gives me the opportunity to help people manifest their hopes, wishes and dreams. I like the world of ideas. I enjoy brainstorming with people about things they want to happen in their lives. Today, I was able to help my massage therapist come up with ideas for ways to build her practice. Later, she dropped me a note in which she said, "Our conversation today felt like a turning point in my life. I felt reassured of always being lovingly guided and protected and was really incredulous over the synchronicity of it all. I am grateful for your validations and suggestions about attracting prosperity and following my heart and my destiny." Who have you been able to help with your guidance and ideas? How did helping someone make you feel? Are you aware of the original source of the ideas that let you assist that individual - where your ideas came from originally?

My Thoughts —

"Discovery is seeing what everybody else has seen and thinking what nobody else has thought."

-- Albert Szent-Gyong

TODAY I HEARD an interview with an author who wrote a book about the Pentagon, and the inner workings of this governmental agency. He said that it is the methodology of Pentagon officials to envision possible wars - ones that they *would* like to happen. He also said they develop funding and weapons to support these *possible* wars, and they gather evidence to *support* the need for the war. I was astounded when I heard this interview. Is this how one section of our government chooses to use their imaginations? Their methodologies support the self-fulfilling prophecy that they are creating their own reality. My imagination chooses to consider the possibility of envisioning peace and how we could go about creating a peaceful world. Do we, as observers of our world, influence what we experience by our thoughts and by our actions? If so, then are we creating wars, poverty, disease and other states of being that result in hardship? Can we envision other possibilities?

My Thoughts —

"When you cease to dream, you cease to live."

-- Malcolm S. Forbes

I REALIZE THAT I have been in a low energy period for too long. In these periods, I find that I cannot stand myself. What I have learned is that I trigger these low rhythms because I am too focused on the external world. I find myself influenced by the financial situation of my business, my relationship with my clients, my health and whether I am happy with my body, concern for my kids getting a good start in their lives, many world situations, and whether my favorite television show is being pre-empted by a sports event. I realize in these moments that I am not connected to my spirit. To reconnect, I spend time in meditation and silent reflection. I use my imagination envisioning what my Spirit would say to me if we were sitting in a room together. What I have learned is that when I am right on the inside, I am right on the outside! What things can you do to reconnect with your Spirit when you feel depressed or lethargic?

My Thoughts —

"Those who preserve their integrity remain unshaken by the storms of daily life. They do not stir like leaves on a tree or follow the herd where it runs. In their mind remains the ideal attitude and conduct of living. This is not something given to them by others. It is their roots and it is their strength that exists deep within them."

-- Anonymous Native American

I MET WITH one of my spiritual teachers today, and I thanked her for helping me find the subtitle to this book. She then spoke with me about how I can manifest my hopes, wishes and dreams. She said I needed to follow my heart in all of my professional and personal pursuits. She asked me, "What do you want in life?" She said that, at a deep level, she sensed my belief system envisioned the world as not being a safe place. She suggested that, in my prayers and meditations, I affirm that I trust Spirit and release any fears that I may have. She said for me to use my imagination and see myself as I desire my world to be, and then walk in such a way that I affirm, with each step, the world as I envision it. I found her advice comforting. Do you have mentors and spiritual teachers who can advise you when you find yourself needing guidance and direction? Remember that people who help you to recognize what is already inside of you are the ones you should work with. They are your holy helpers!

My Thoughts —

"I have heard it said that the first ingredient of success — the earliest spark in the dreaming youth - is this: dream a great dream."

-- John Alan Appleman

YESTERDAY, I NEEDED to leave the house to go to an appointment, but I couldn't find my car keys. I looked everywhere, all the while becoming more and more agitated. I finally had to take our old pickup truck in order to get to the appointment on time. As I was driving, I began to try to imagine how I might find my keys. My inner voice said, "Ask Spirit," so I asked my spirit to show me where the keys were. A few miles down the road, a picture came into my mind - I saw a plastic box in the top of my closet, which I thought was an odd thing to be imagining. When I returned home and went to the closet, I pulled the plastic box down from the shelf, and inside it were my keys. I had been putting away some materials earlier in the morning, and must have thown my keys in the box by mistake. I offer this story to you to show that the power of our imagination is incredible when we ask - and when we pay attention to the answer!

My Thoughts —

"The new hero is the innovator."

-- Alvin Toffler

TODAY, AT A workshop, I heard someone talking about imagination, and she reminded me of my belief in the power of the imaginative process. She said that the mind is the creative agent of the universe. The mind is the extension of the soul, which is the divine mind. Her remarks reminded me that our imaginations are a conduit to the very power which created the universe as we know it. This all-loving and all-powerful force had something in its imagination for us to discover. By discovering our spirit, we discover this intelligent force. Although there are many names for this source, I believe that there is only one source. How do you think this force really sees you? And if you are part of this source, how do you see yourself? We are all on a journey to discover the truth of our being, and when you find the truth - and you will know it when you do - then you will know where your hopes, wishes and dreams truly reside.

My Thoughts —

"Why must we believe? Because God is belief...and belief is Law, and Law produces form, in substance."

-- Ernest Holmes

CHAPTER THREE

CORE DESIRE

"Nothing can happen to us that is not first an accepted belief in our own consciousness."

-- Ernest Holmes

CORE DESIRE

(Core n. center, nucleus, heart, essence, root.)
(Desire n. want, longing, hunger, passion, fervor, urge.)

SEVERAL YEARS AGO, a well-known motivational speaker came to San Antonio to deliver a one-day seminar on the power of goal-setting. Over two hundred people – who had been anticipating his visit for weeks - attended the session.

After speaking the entire day, the motivational speaker said goodbye to everyone and started to leave the stage when a bright-eyed young man in his twenties came up to the stage and began conversing with the speaker. The young man passionately told the speaker that he felt motivated and inspired to help people as a result of what he heard that day.

He asked the speaker if he could teach him how to set up a business on motivational speaking. Though the speaker was tired from having taught all day, the young man's enthusiasm was so convincing that the speaker sat down with the young man and spent the next hour giving him suggestions on how to start his own business.

Finally, when the speaker had given the young man all the ideas he had on starting a business, he sent the young man on his way. "I felt totally drained," he told me, "but I felt good about helping this young man get started in life with something he felt was his core desire." And in return, the young man had assured the speaker that he would put his mentoring to good use.

About a year later, the motivational speaker came back to San Antonio to deliver another seminar, and while speaking, he noticed a familiar face in the crowd of attendees. It was the young man he had mentored a year earlier. At the break, the speaker went over to the young man ready to hear a wonderful success story.

He asked the young man how he was doing with his business, and with an embarrassed frown, the young man remarked that he had not even started to do anything to create his motivational business. The speaker looked at the young man and told him that, clearly, having his own motivational business had not been a *core desire* after all.

You see, the speaker, in his tutelage of this young man, had explained that everything that a person attracts in their life is a result of the power of a core desire. All wishes and desires become manifest because of the person's deep desire to *make* them happen.

He advised the young man to keep searching for his core desire because, when he found it, he would discover that nothing would keep him from acting on and manifesting that desire.

How DEEPLY DO you want to live the best life you possibly can? How much do you want financial independence? Do you believe in perfect health and do you want to develop the habits to keep yourself in good shape? How badly do you want a true soul-connected relationship with someone? Do you desire a rewarding and fulfilling career? Do you want peace on this planet?

Your answer to most of these questions is probably a clear *yes*. But the problem is that the patterns of our habits and our thoughts oftentimes get in the way of our desires. We may struggle with staying on our diets, or we may be tempted to overuse our credit cards. Why, when we truly want something deeply, do we allow our habits and old patterns to sabotage what we really want?

The answer is that if what we want is not a *core desire*, then we may not be able to prevent old habits and patterns from interfering with our goal. My contention is that if a person is not in touch with their spirit, then they will allow their long-time habits to control them.

The key to making changes in our lives is *understanding that we control our thoughts*. Unfortunately, many of us allow our thoughts to control us. When you are working from your *core*, you are living your life from your essence, your spirit. When you are acting on your *desire*, then you create your intention to attract the very thing you want.

You are a soul connected to the very power that created this universe. Your capabilities are unlimited. When you desire something, you first must see and feel it in your imagination(and your heart!). The next step is to decide how much you really want it, and if you want it intensely, to act on it. If you follow this pattern – to see it and feel it in your imagination, to determine if you want it intensely, and then to act on that desire - you are truly working with a core desire.

Core desires should be something *you* really want - not what someone else tells you to want. Core desires are not triggered by external influences, but manifest from within. When you are connected with your spirit, then core desires are not chores. They are filled with joy, anticipation, and gratitude because you understand that you can create anything you desire if you truly believe in it.

ACTION STEP

IN THE LAST chapter, you chose an area from your *Life Impact Areas* that you took into your imagination, envisioning the very thing you desired manifesting in your life. Now, find a quiet spot where you can be alone. Close your eyes and envision what you desire, just as you did in the last chapter. Now ask yourself these questions: How deeply do you want this to happen? Take this feeling – the power of it - into your heart. The next question is a tough one: How much are you willing to risk to make what you desire happen? Are you willing to risk everything? Finally, ask yourself the ultimate question: Does your desire feel in tune with your spirit? In other words, using your intuition, does your spirit say *yes* to you about this desire, or does it caution you with a *no*? Remember -you are a co-creator, partnered with the most intelligent force in the universe. You are not alone in your decision-making! Write down in a journal the impressions you received during this action step and we will review them throughout this book.

AFFIRMATION

My mind and heart are enormously powerful. Through my mind and heart, I am connected with the Divine Power, and this loving force listens and responds to my every need.

As a soul, you eventually come to the conclusion that life is about making choices and taking actions that will contribute to the evolvement of your soul. With this in mind, are there experiences you would like to have, but have not yet had? If you knew that next week you would be making your transition from this world, would there be any regrets that you had regarding something you wish you had done, but did not? If there are things you would like to experience, or things left undone in your life, then let these desires become core desires for you. Choose what you want to bring into your life. Imagine it. Then act on it, knowing that you are advancing the development of your soul. Each moment affords us the opportunity to gain experience in our lives.

My Thoughts —

"It has long since come to my attention that people of accomplishment rarely sat back and let things happen to them. They went out and happened to things."

-- Leonardo da Vinci

RECENTLY I FOUND myself looking back at the success of my training and consulting business, and searching for the common denominator which made it so. What I have discovered about my success is that I am very passionate about what I do. I sincerely enjoy helping others improve their lives. I am driven to explore the spiritual dimensions of my consciousness, and I find deep satisfaction in sharing my journey with others, in the hope that my own journey will help others in their lives. My passion is driven by my core desire. I have found what turns me on. The grand secret to my revelations about my professional and personal pursuits and successes is that my core desire originates from within me. I know this because when I am struggling with my clients I notice that I am not deterred from my mission. Have you determined what your core desires are? What are you passionate about? Have you found a sense of purpose in your life?

My Thoughts —

"The strong passion for any object will ensure success, for the desire of the end will point out the means."

-- Ben Stein

I AM ENJOYING developing a new workshop called *Core Training*. The word "Core" means the center, the heart, and the essence. I like the word, and it origins, because to me it represents the magic of how goals are attained. Goals are attained, and become realized, because all things and all ideas come from Source. An idea you have comes from the very intelligence that created the universe. When you realize that everything does come from Spirit, then you begin to understand how all of your hopes, wishes, and dreams can be manifested. The interesting insight that I have discovered in my research for the Core Training workshop is that we live in a universe that responds to thought. By stating and writing down your intention, by imagining the very thing you want and by acting on it, you set all of these factors into motion, and the universe responds by bringing your idea into physical creation. The key is to develop a deep yearning for your desire – your core desire, the desire that comes from within you.

My Thoughts —

"I am for everything starting into full-blown perfection at once."

-- Susan Edmondstone Ferrier

LAST YEAR I developed a new workshop called *Adventures in Self-Management.* It's a stress management workshop that helps people understand what stress is, and how stress manifests in one's life. The workshop has been a huge success, both in terms of student response, and in terms of its positive financial impact on my business. As I have watched the success of this workshop develop, I have become very intrigued by the creative process. I find taking an idea, developing it, and putting it into action to be an enthralling process. There were a number of factors that contributed to the success of this workshop. I enjoy teaching it, and I found the workshop was fun to facilitate. Additionally, I'm inspired by people's reactions to the workshop. This workshop's content – and its potential to change people's lives - inspired me, and as a result, developing it became a core desire for me. That initial passion for the work itself – rather than for the money it could generate for me – led naturally to a financially successful venture. Do you, too, have an idea that you deeply believe in, and are you willing to do what it takes to put that idea into action?

My Thoughts —

"No matter what we feel or know, no matter what our potential gifts or talents, only action brings them to life."

--Dan Millman

WHEN I AM working with my clients, I look for one significant characteristic in each of them. I try to determine whether they are in connection with their spirit, or are not. Regardless of whether they are in connection with their spirit or not, they are creating the circumstances of their lives. I have found that not everyone understands what it means to be in connection with Spirit. If a person is not enjoying life, they are out of connection. If they are experiencing financial issues, career or relationship challenges, they are out of connection with their spirit. So I teach people how to recognize their spirit and live their lives from their spirit. Doing so is not always easy, as we have many habits and temptations that lure us away from spirit. But I do share with people my own approach - that my core desire each day is to know my spirit in each moment and live my life in connection with source. I confess that, on some days, I do well; on others, I learn from the gifts of the challenges I attract to myself.

My Thoughts —

"All know the way, few actually walk it."

--Bodhidharm

READERS HAVE OFFERED me different opinions on my first two books. Many say they enjoyed reading them, and have told me that the books challenged them to take a deeper look at their lives; I find that response very fulfilling. Other readers have said my writings are in conflict with their personal philosophies, and I've found that response to be more of a challenge. These readers often have adamant beliefs about God, and some have found my writings disconcerting, and have assured me that they are praying for my soul. In the face of such objections, I find I must draw upon my courage to continue to write about my truths, and hope that my own approach to spirituality will help people clarify their own belief system. What I have learned from people who disagree with my approach is that, because my writings reflect my core desires, I am not swayed by opinions that diverge from my own. Ultimately, our lives are reflection of our understanding and application of our truths and our values; I cannot judge others based on how they choose to live their lives, or based on what they believe. I can only hope my writings offer people the chance to evaluate their own beliefs, and reflect on what is important in their lives.

My Thoughts —

"Know what's most important and give it all you've got."

-- Lee Iacocca

I WAS WATCHING the movie THE SHAWSHANK REDEMPTION and took note when one of the characters remarked, "Get busy livin' or get busy dyin!" I love this quote, because I believe that each soul has that very choice. We are either living our lives with passion and enthusiasm, or we are traveling through life with no sense of purpose or enjoyment. How do you feel about your own life? Do you have the sense that your existence has a purpose? If you do, then you have found your core desire. Finding your core desire is not the answer to eternal happiness – it won't exclude you from the many life challenges that any worthwhile life attracts. But it does mean you will see and react to life's challenges differently because you are in touch with your core desires and your spirit. We live in a world that reflects our thoughts, our words, and our actions. We live in a world that is a reflection of what is happening inside of us. We can either choose to embrace life, or we can choose to be victims who blame others for our unhappiness.

My Thoughts —

"The question is: who will go to heaven first - the person who talks or the person who acts?"

-- Author Unknown

ONE OF THE basic tenets of this book is this: *all creation begins with an idea*. For example, the book you are currently reading is the third book in the Practical Spirituality series, and I have several more books outlined in this series. All of these books began with an idea in my imagination. I chose as a soul to envision these books in my consciousness, and then I had to ask myself whether I REALLY wanted to write them, get them published and market them. With the time and expense involved in writing and marketing these books, I can assure you that, if they were not core desires, they would never have been completed and published. I work with a number of clients who have great ideas, but they lack the passion it takes to bring those ideas to fruition. When you find your essence and your core, staying the course until your dreams become reality will no longer be a challenge. You will wake up every day yearning to bring your idea into creation because you understand that the universe withholds nothing from us. Nothing! What does this dynamic mean to you? It means all of your hopes, wishes and desires are only waiting for your imagination to provide the passion, and for you to choose to *do* something with your idea. You will do something, and see your idea through, if it is a core desire.

My Thoughts —

"No, you never get any fun out of things you haven't done."

-- Ogden Nash

57

I RECENTLY EXPERIENCED a bit of a lull in my business, in which I did not do much training and consulting. These lulls are partly the natural rhythm of my business, and partly caused by my desire to relax and renew my energy before the next wave of business. I've learned, during these lulls, that the opportunity to rest and reflect is wonderful – but that, unfortunately, during these periods my bills exceed my income. What I have learned over the years is to take advantage of these periods, not only to recuperate but to stay creative. I've learned that, once I do get busy again, I won't have as much time to work on my books or new workshops. So I have learned to make the most of the free time, and to trust during these periods that my business will pick up - which it *always* has and always will! I can be assured my business will pick up again because my business and my life are reflections of my core desires. Spirit knows what I desire, and I live my life with total confidence that all my hopes, wishes, and desires have already been fulfilled. This confidence comes from a place deep inside of myself — my core — and I have the wonderful opportunity to share my journey with those who read my books or take my workshops.

My Thoughts —

"All things are possible to one who believes."

--Saint Bernard of Clairvaux

TODAY I FOUND myself journaling about how quiet my life has been over the past few weeks – how little seems to be going on in my life. Usually my life is bustling - there are synchronicities, chance encounters, key phrases in songs I'm listening to that provide inspiration, or people calling unexpectedly. These quiet periods are hard, because it seems I have nothing to write about when it feels as though there is really nothing going on. This morning, as I journaled, I thought to myself, "Does Spirit take off during these times and leave me alone?" I find myself challenged during these times, and those challenges offer me the opportunity to look closely at my core desires. The reality is that Spirit does not take time off. If I don't spot the positive things going on in my life, it's because I am just not paying attention to what is going on around me or inside of myself. My life always gives me things to be grateful for, and I can always find the opportunity to help someone, even if it just means opening a door for someone else. I need to keep my focus, pay attention, and look for opportunities to serve; in doing so, I stay in contact with my core desires and my spirit.

My Thoughts —

"For the ordinary business of life, an ounce
of habit is worth a pound of intellect."

-- Thomas B. Reed

CHAPTER FOUR

VISION

"The empires of the future are empires of the mind."

-- Winston Churchill

VISION

(n. seeing, perception, revelation, idea, mental image, foresight)

My WIFE IS an elementary principal of a Title I school in San Antonio, Texas. Title I schools are those in which children in low-income communities are at risk of school failure. Often, the risk of failure is increased due to the economic status of the parents, and by children being raised by single parents or an extended family member. Many parents whose children attend Title I schools never finished school themselves, and are often trying to get by in low paying jobs.

The percentage of kids at risk varies depending upon the number of parents who are struggling economically. For my wife's school, ninety-eight percent of the student population is at risk for school failure.

My wife's school district hired her in the year 2000 to take over her current school and charged her with turning the school around. At that time, the school was on the verge of being taken over by the Texas Education Agency because of its students' poor test scores.

Her first year was quite challenging. Teacher morale was low. The curriculum in reading, writing, and math was inconsistent. Leadership of the school had been lacking, and parents felt they were unwelcome at the school. This elementary school had been built in 1960, and the building and classrooms were deteriorating.

Understanding what my wife encountered when she was brought into this situation will help you to appreciate how far her school has come since then. When she took over the school in 2000, many of the good teachers were burnt out. Overall, the staff members had very negative attitudes. The children had numerous discipline problems, there was a great deal of infighting among the teachers, and the parents had little involvement with the school.

Then, in 2001, the school district took a very courageous step and reconstituted my wife's school. Under this approach, all the teachers had to reapply for their jobs. Any teacher not rehired was assigned to another school in the district. As you can imagine, this was a stressful time for the school, the staff, and the kids. By the time the reconstitution was complete, my wife had replaced over seventy-five percent of her staff with new teachers.

I watched in awe as my wife went to work each day with the task of not only training the new staff, but also training the old staff on how to integrate a consistent curriculum in the school. My wife broke the staff members into small groups and developed an initial five-year vision for the school.

This five-year vision was designed to build a community of learners and develop relationships between the kids, the staff, the parents and the community. The plan included high-caliber professional development for the teachers to help them understand the "art" of their craft. Of particular importance was helping the teachers and parents comprehend that all of these kids have potential, regardless of their backgrounds.

The results have been amazing. There are many cultures and languages spoken at my wife's school – all have made significant progress. Since the reconstitution, discipline referrals are down, parents are more involved, test scores have improved even as testing standards have risen, and there has been minimal teacher turnover. Teachers have become more proficient. The local community businesses have become more involved by offering financial assistance and participating in mentor programs for the students. The central office has been extremely supportive because of the positive changes they have seen at the school.

All this is made even more impressive when you consider the complexity of running a public school. I have trained many principals in my consulting business, and I have found that the job of principal is the most complex of any position I train in the corporate and educational world.

Though the improvements have been remarkable, my wife's role as a leader in the school – and the resulting stress and new challenges – are ongoing. With the *No Child Left Behind* act, legislation has put enormous pressures on Title I schools. I watch my wife's teachers work with this at-risk population and I am amazed at their resiliency. What keeps my wife from burning out? What keeps her teachers from wanting to leave and go to more affluent schools where the challenges are more manageable?

The answer is that my wife brought a clear and inspiring *vision* to her school. She got everyone involved – teachers, parents, school district representatives, area businesses and students - and created a collaborative atmosphere. The welfare of the kids became the unifying focus.

Her vision described where they were beginning and where they needed to go. She laid out what professional training would be given to support the process. She set up communication structures within the school to monitor the pulse of her staff and keep track of their needs.

As a result, parents have become more involved - not only at school, but at home with their kids as well. My wife has been told that parents feel more welcomed at school and, most importantly, they have noticed their kids are happier and feel supported and loved by the school staff.

There are still many daily challenges at my wife's school. Some of her kids are exposed to such poor home environments that they are cared for better at school than they are home. But the important point here is that the vision has changed at her school. The vision is no longer the responsibility of the principal, but the responsibility of all parties, from parents to teachers to students. The vision has become the "boss".

I BELIEVE THAT there is a passage in Proverb that says, "Where there is no vision, the people perish." Up to this point, I have suggested that you imagine what you want in your life. I have asked you to consider whether what you want is really a core desire. In other words, are you willing to risk everything to attract your hopes, wishes or desires?

But now the concept of *vision* enters in. Vision shows us how to attract our goals, whatever they are. When you have vision you are literally aligning desire with your divinity. As a soul, you are given the power to choose, and that choice dictates that you can bring into your life anything you desire. The key is to hold the vision for your desire in your consciousness, until it manifests.

According to Quantum Physicists, we create our reality by our focus and intention. They believe that energy follows thought and that our thoughts come into formation by what we put our attention on. Therefore, the power of vision coalesces our very thoughts. Our job is to keep our focus and be able to carry our vision in our thoughts as we observe our external world beginning to take shape according to our vision and our image.

Think of a vision as a roadmap, similar to one you might use if you were going to take a trip. You imagine your destination, and along the way while enjoying the scenery - you still are holding the end result or destination in your consciousness.

The key point for you to understand is that the visioning process must take place first in our consciousness, or inside of us. It is important that you keep this in mind, because nothing happens outside of ourselves that does not first begin inside of us. Inside your consciousness is the source of your power. It is the launching pad for your hopes, wishes and dreams. So I ask you, now: what is your vision for your life? If you can visualize it and believe in it, and if you take the proper action steps, then all of your hopes, wishes and dreams can be realized.

ACTION STEP

MANY TIMES WHEN we watch a movie, we find ourselves being drawn into the story because we are imagining how *we* would react to the plot that is unfolding before our eyes; and sometimes the film reminds us of something that has happened in our own lives. In this action step, you are going to create a movie and *step into that movie*. Find a quiet, private spot. With your eyes closed, imagine your desire (what you have chosen in your *Life Impact Area*) playing out before you with you actually participating in whatever you have wished for. Make it very kinesthetic. For example, if you see yourself walking on a beach, actually feel your feet pressing into the sand, and feel the wind blowing on your face. After you have envisioned your desire, then open your eyes and spend the rest of your day holding that vision in your awareness. As you go through your day, see your desire as having already manifested. Hold this vision for your desire each day until what your desire manifests – and it will.

AFFIRMATION

In each moment, I am holding the vision for my deepest desires in my awareness. I am a soul, and I am a divine being, and all that I desire is already coming into my life.

IF YOU HAVE participated in a prayer group – a group that holds in their consciousness the highest good for a person, group or nation – you know the power of *vision*. A prayer group holds a vision of what they pray to be. They will not hold vision of healing, for example, but rather a vision of the person already healed. The group will not ask for financial help for someone they pray for, but rather will envision the person as being prosperous. This is the power of visioning – to manifest what we wish. It is important for you to hold such a vision for your own life, seeing everything you desire as being already complete, already a reality. For in fact, it already is - if you can envision it. Please also be aware that when you vision, you are first doing so inside your consciousness. Then, from within your own consciousness and imagination, walk through your daily affairs holding the vision for your desire as if you already have it. Soon you will!

My Thoughts —

Chance favors the prepared mind."

-- Louis Pasteur

I TOLD MY workshop students today that, when I teach, I expect to reach everyone with the purpose and intent of my instruction. They thought that my expectations were too high because they felt not everyone will follow through with instructions they are given. With the past history of observing some of my clients after they have taken my instruction, I would agree that not everyone will practice what I teach. My point, though, was that the *vision* I hold encompasses everyone. I believe that, if I reach just one person, that change is substantial, and that connection is a major accomplishment. What I learned from this dialogue with my class today was to have the courage and the steadfastness to envision reaching the greatest number people, regardless of the size of my audience.

My Thoughts —

"The idea is to seek a vision that gives you purpose in life and then to implement that vision."

-- Lewis P. Johnson

Do YOU HAVE a vision for your own life? It is important for you to understand that vision drives attitude. Life has meaning when you have a vision for your life. When you have a vision, you perceive life differently than those who do not, because you find a unifying purpose in everything you do. You see, vision controls our perceptions, and our perceptions control our reality. What would your life reflect if part of the vision you held for yourself included the perfect career, financial prosperity, loving relationships, and perfect health?

My Thoughts —

"The appetite grows by what it feeds on."

-- Albert D. Richardson

David D. Dameron

HERE IS A verbatim reminder that I wrote in my daily journal a few years ago: "I am an individualized aspect of the Divine - a concentrated center of spiritual energy. Within my energy field, I have different vibrations. The higher I raise my frequency through positive thoughts, the higher my vibration. The higher my vibration, the more I bring into being the power of my divine nature. Everything I desire is already manifest. When I believe this, imagine this, and feel this, then it becomes manifest in a physical way. When I desire something, I give thanks for that which is happening in my life. I am lacking nothing in my life. This is the vision that I hold for my life."

My Thoughts —

"Clarity of mind, body, and spirit is the key to creativity."

-- Dan Wakefield

I WAS PLAYING a game on my computer this evening when I noticed what a good mood I was in. I hadn't had any luck at winning the game, and on a whim, I decided to envision winning the next round – and I did win! I went on to win four times in a row. Whether winning a computer game or achieving a major goal in my life, I remain in awe of the power of vision, and what is possible when I feel really connected to my spirit. I am learning how to take this feeling and possibility into all areas of my life. I realized what is possible if I can hold onto this vibration, this positive understanding of my own potential. That is my challenge – to remember that my vision creates my reality. I am reminded in each moment to hold in my consciousness the desired outcome that I envision. This is the true power of vision!

My Thoughts —

"Our aspirations are our possibilities."

--Robert Browning

I CONTINUE TO find the work of quantum physicists quite intriguing. These pioneers continue to discover ways in which particles of energy respond to our focus. Whatever we put our focus on is what directs matter to form to that image. Therefore, if you want something new in your life or you wish to attract what you desire, all you have to do is redirect your focus to the desired outcome. I am intrigued by this idea because it means that, no matter what we have created in the past, what we have created can be altered by redirecting our focus. This is the power of holding the vision for what we desire. The challenge is to hold the focus until the desired outcome manifests. The implications of visioning are huge, not only for our own lives but for what we can create on this planet: peace, prosperity, abundance, respect, and an honoring of diversity.

My Thoughts —

"The sea is always the same and yet the sea always changes."

-- Carl Sandburg

I RAN ACROSS an old journal entry of mine from twenty-five years ago, and it reminded me of the importance of vision in our lives: "Creation is complete. I see the divine blueprint when I look at a mustard seed. This small seed has within it the blueprint it needs to evolve into its designed potential: a mustard plant. It cannot become anything else. Yet, in our humanity, we fight to be something else, trying to control our lives through our egos when our blueprint contains our divine destiny. Why do we deny who we really are? Why do we create anything else but love, joy, and compassion? I am reminded to embrace my divinity on a daily basis, and I remind myself that I am a part of the divine vision and plan for my life."

My Thoughts —

"Our reach should exceed our grasp, or what's heaven for?"

-- Robert Browning

I HAVE TO be honest and admit to you that there are times I am insecure about what I'm writing about. Often, while I work, I wonder whether people will appreciate or understand my viewpoint. Will I be accepted or rejected by the public? I shared these doubts with my wife, and she gently reminded me of the number of people who have responded positively to my books. She said that I must not fail my vision by always needing positive feedback, or by worrying about negative reactions from people. She said I must have courage to believe in my vision and know that if even one person is changed by what I write, my books have served their purpose. I am glad I have my wife to remind me of the power of vision.

My Thoughts —

"Make it new."

--Ezra Pound

TODAY, IN A workshop, I was asked a very profound question: what is the highest thought I could have about myself? The workshop facilitator then told me to figure out the answer to that question - and live it. The question took me directly to the core of my being, and I acknowledged that I am a divine being. Living this insight on a daily basis remains a constant challenge for me, but the road of perseverance has led me to place where, at times, I feel a peace that surpasses all understanding. So I ask you: what is the highest thought you could have about yourself? I ask you to reach for the answer to that question, and then I invite you to live it. This is the power of having a vision.

My Thoughts —

"The mind is capable of anything, because everything is in it - all the past, as well as the future."

--Author unknown

TODAY I HAVE been experiencing some anxiety about my son and the question of whether he would find a good job after he graduates from college. In what town would he end up living? What challenges would he encounter, out on his own? As I was having the usual parental anxieties, I recalled that I knew how to manifest what I desired, by holding my vision for my son for his highest good. Playing the "what if" game was only limiting the energy that could be brought to the situation. I turned to envisioning his highest good, and, as it turned out, my son was hired by an excellent company, and is adapting well to being on his own. I continue to hold a loving vision for my son's happiness. I also realize that it is important for him to make that same choice for himself if he chooses to!

My Thoughts —

"Tomorrow belongs to those who have vision today."

-- Author unknown

CHAPTER FIVE

INTENTION

"High achievement always takes place in the framework of high expectation."

-- Jack and Garry Kinder

INTENTION

(n. purpose, intent, goal, aim, design, plan, end, target)

IN THE LATE 1980s, I reached a very special point in my life at which – although I had done a great deal of spiritual work – I found myself without spiritual resources to sustain me. My external world did not look like I had planned it. I was going through a divorce, my professional pursuits were not satisfying, and my financial situation looked bleak. To put it bluntly, I did not feel comfortable with my spiritual pursuits anymore.

I've found I sink into these spiritual low points from time to time. When I do, I end up responding as I did this time – by breaking down and, in privacy, letting my frustrations out. Between yelling, screaming, crying, and even throwing things, I pretty much told whoever was listening - even though I was by myself - that my current situation was unacceptable.

I went over the last six or seven years, noting that I had done everything I should have done. I had followed my guidance and risked everything to understand who God was and to understand the purpose of my life. In this time of doubt, I made an effort to reaffirm that I was a divine being, and that I was entitled to prosperity and abundance, a fulfilling career and a satisfying relationship.

After my tirade (which lasted for most of the day), I finally sat down in silence, and I heard a small voice in my head say, "State your intentions." Recognizing this voice as a voice of my own destiny, of spirit, I grabbed a piece of paper and wrote down four intentions:

1. I desire to have my own professional training and consulting business.

2. I desire financial freedom, with my revenue always exceeding my expenses.

3. I desire a soul-connected relationship and life partner.

4. I desire to manifest my divine potential.

I DIDN'T PLAY with the wording of my statements – I wasn't interested in word craft. I just wrote what I was feeling. I then re-stated these intentions as I meditated. As I meditated, I imagined what my life would look like – and how I would feel – when they manifested.

My little voice said to me, "*It is done.*" I was surprised by this message – at first, when I opened my eyes, it brought to mind the world that I wanted to leave behind. But then I knew what *it is done* meant. It meant that what I desired has already been given to me. I just needed to be patient, wait on the will of heaven, and begin acting on my intentions.

Since that time I have learned many things about my four intentions. Each has manifested in its own way, and each continues to unfold. I have a very successful training and consulting business. Almost immediately, my revenue from my business began to exceed my expenses. I found my soul-mate who I wrote about in my second book.

The last intention – that I manifest my divine potential - continues to be a work in progress, and I have discovered it always will be. Closing the gap between my personality and ego and my divine nature is what I believe to be the primary purpose of my life. In the years since I listed this intention, I have learned that, in acknowledging my desire to unfold my divinity, I sent out that intention. Spirit and the universe responded - on a daily basis, I can assure you that I have many opportunities to choose between my ego and my spirit.

INTENTION BEGINS THE process of putting your hopes, wishes and dreams into action. Up to this point in Stage One, we have been preparing the foundation for the launch of your idea. With intention, you are defining what you want, much as you would when ordering something from a mail order catalog. It is like getting on the telephone and requesting something you desire, which in this case is something from your **Life Impact Areas**.

Intention is like using a magnifying glass to direct your mind with a clear purpose toward an outcome you are hoping for. It is the same intent you rely on when you are throwing a pair of dice in a game, flipping a coin and calling heads or tails, or shooting a basketball in a game of "horse" with someone.

You may have focused your intent for years without even thinking about it or being aware of it. It may have come naturally to you, or you may have been taught to do it. But when focused in a *conscious* way, the power of intention manifests quite differently. With the power of your thoughts and your focus, and with proper action, you are affirming to life your intention. You are bringing such incredible energy to your intention that life goes to work to bring you the very thing you desire.

As a soul, you have the power to choose your intention. But I also want to emphasize that you are more than a soul. You are a divine being, imbued with a co-creative power that is connected to the very source that created the entire universe. Now that's powerful! The magnitude of this energy is directly connected to your belief that you are creating everything in your life with your thoughts, words, and actions, and in relationship with the very power that created the world you live in.

ACTION STEP

As a PRELIMINARY step prior to beginning Stage Two in the next chapter, sit quietly in a chair and, in privacy, close your eyes, and take nine deep breaths - breathing from your stomach, your diaphragm. After, you have taken nine breaths, visualize the idea you have chosen from you *Life Impact Area,* and take that picture into the area of your heart. Feel the joy of attracting the desire you have chosen. Decide you are going to manifest your desire. Express gratitude for having that desire manifest in your life. Hold on to this feeling for a few minutes and then open your eyes. Now your intention for your hope, wish and dream is ready to be launched in Stage Two.

AFFIRMATION

I create my world in collaboration with my spirit. As I become more conscious of my divinity, I am willing to risk, and I effectively plan, act on, and manifest whatever I desire in life. This is my intention.

I WENT TO a meeting last week, and I was listening to one of the participants, who was putting out chairs. She was saying to herself, "I will put out only ten chairs even though the room holds twenty. And if more people come, I'll put out more chairs." I commented to her that if she put out more chairs, maybe more people would come. At first, she did not understand what I meant, but then she smiled and seemed to understand. She then put out all twenty chairs – and that night twenty people showed up. This episode reminded me of intention, and what can manifest is you choose not to limit spirit. I chose in this instance not to set a limit on what I desired to see manifested. We need to create space for expansion in our lives. So in each moment, I look at my intentions and make sure they are broad enough to allow Spirit to fulfill my desires.

My Thoughts —

"Expect the best"

-- Joe Batten

TODAY, WHILE DRIVING, I found myself reviewing the intentions I have set for the coming year. I have really challenged myself to improve in several areas of my life, and accordingly, I am setting some business goals that are quite formidable. As I began to question whether I had been too ambitious with my goals for the year, I saw a lighted sign along the highway that said, "Anything is possible." This sign was a nice reminder from Spirit, telling me that if I can conceive it and believe in it, then, truly, anything is possible. Can you define your intentions for your life? Do you truly believe in them? Are you willing to take the steps to manifest your intentions?

My Thoughts —

*"All dreams can come true – if we have
the courage to pursue them."*

-- Walt Disney

I WAS ASKED today to explain the difference between a core desire and an intention. I told the person asking me that a core desire is something that you have identified as being really desirable in your life. Intention is the willingness to *act* on that desire. Core desires do not happen unless you act on them. Intention is the final internal step that you take in your mind to say, "I am now ready to bring my desire into my life." Using our imagination, holding our vision, and getting ready to act on our intention are all processes that occur within us first. This is the grand secret of how things manifest in our lives. They originate from the inside!

My Thoughts —

"Don't sit down and wait for opportunities to come, you have to get up and make them."

-- Madame C.J. Walker

THERE IS A tendency when setting an intention or a goal to force something to happen. I was reminded of this when I read in my journal an entry I had written in 2003. "Take advantage of my halts. The nature of my journey depends upon my attitude. Clarity of my intention and my will are important at this stage. Do not act hastily. Wait for the will of heaven. Do not go beyond that which has not yet begun." This journal entry was a direct insight into a project on which I was working. I learned from this entry not to push the doors open, but to let them open. I have to retrain myself to understand this concept – it has been my approach to push the doors open to make something happen, but heaven works in its own time.

My Thoughts —

"Nature imitates herself: A grain thrown into good ground brings forth fruit; a principle thrown into a good mind brings forth fruit."

-- Blaise Pascal

89

WHEN YOU SET forth an intention, you are literally sending out a form of energy that affects things, even at great distances. For example, science knows through experiments that when a dog's owner decides to come home, the animal will pick up this intention and show excitement, even before its owner arrives. How many times has someone called you when you just happen to be thinking of him or her? How many times has a person given you a piece of information about something for which you were searching? These are not chance incidents. The power of your intentions is enormous. Be cognizant of what you are thinking, what you are saying, and what actions you are taking.

My Thoughts —

"The act of acting morally is behaving as if everything we do matters."

-- Gloria Steinem

I RECENTLY ADDED a new service called Master Training to my training and consulting business. The intent of this service is to work with individuals one-on-one, helping them focus on particular areas of their lives where they want to make improvements. I sent an email to my clients to announce the new service and, to my amazement, I landed three clients right away. When I looked at the response to my intention, I realized that one of the reasons my intentions manifest is that I am very passionate about my work. I believe that passion supports my intention and, like a magnet, attracts whatever is necessary to manifest my desire. I also believe in the importance of my work. What are you passionate about?

My Thoughts —

*"Your future depends upon many things,
but mostly on you."*

-- Frank Tyger

I RECENTLY TRAINED adults working at an elementary school, and, in the process of training them, I began to wonder whether my training – the approaches and suggestions I made - was really being accepted. The participants showed a lot of resistance at first to what I was trying to teach them. But I was asked to return and give them additional training, and when I did, I noticed a completely different attitude on the part of the participants. What I learned from this experience was to never question whether what I am doing is having an effect. My intention is to provide information that will help people improve their lives if they practice what I am showing them. I must remind myself to hold a vision of receptivity on the part of the participants, and I must teach with the confidence that if even one person makes a change in their life, then I have accomplished my intention.

My Thoughts —

"True richness is made day by day, with great effort."

-- Francesco Alberoni

I REALIZED TODAY that all the material things I use in my life, each and every day, were a product of someone's intention. The chair I sit in or the car I drive were ideas created in someone's imagination; through labor and hard work, those ideas were brought into creation. We are creative beings, and our lives are a reflection of our intention. Just as an artist paints a picture on a canvas, we are creating our world through the power of our intentions. Therefore, it would behoove us to be clear about what we desire and to be cognizant of our actions, because whatever intention we embark upon is what we create in our lives. It would be of great benefit to you to consider the possibilities that are available to you through approaching life with proper intentions.

My Thoughts —

"I have made my world and it is a much better world than I ever saw outside."

-- Louise Nevelson

ONE OF THE companies that I have worked with for years recently went public, and I was told over one hundred executives in the company became millionaires as a result. As my wife and I were discussing this, I remarked how happy I was for those one hundred individuals because I believe that they were manifesting their divine abundance. This abundance is available to all of us, and we attract it in different ways. But if you look underneath the surface, you will discover that prosperous people are intentional in their approach to life. We all have access to infinite prosperity, and part of life is learning to decipher the code to access that infinite abundance. The power of intention is one of the magnets that attracts prosperity to us. Realizing our intention functions as a magnet is one of the keys to attracting our divine inheritance.

My Thoughts —

"Everyone take heart, it'll be a good year."

-- Peter Breinholt

I GREW UP listening to my parents preach to me that the only way you make it in life is through hard work. That was their belief, and the way in which they saw the world. But in later years, I learned a higher truth for myself. I now see life as an *invitation*. I invite spirit into my life. I invite my hopes, wishes and dreams. I no longer exert my will to achieve what I desire in my life - because I have learned that what I desire has already been given to me. The actions I take to bring my intention into my life are only to assist the birth of my idea into creation. I am like a midwife delivering my intention. I have learned to relax more with my goals and intentions, and I am discovering how to wait on the will of heaven. Soon, I am shown what actions I must take. I understand what a hard concept this will be to understand if you were brought up to "work by the sweat of the brow," as my parents suggested. But if you can shift your focus, I promise you, you will realize your dreams.

My Thoughts —

"I know absolutely nothing. That is why each new day, each new moment, is truly an adventure."

-- Ross Fields

STAGE TWO

FEEL THE FEELING

"The heart has always been a symbol of love, courage, and devotion. Heart and Soul are two words often found together and for good reason. It is through the heart that the soul expresses itself. The heart is the organ that keeps us alive physically, and it is the central source of our emotions and feelings."

-- Terry Lynn Taylor
and Mary Beth Crain
from ANGEL WISDOM

FEELING

(n.sensation, experience, perception, consciousness, emotion, passion, heart, belief)

THE GRAND SECRET for why things happen in our lives lies within the pages that follow. They explain the dynamic that all the things you accomplish in your life rely on one key element: your strong feelings. Think about this. Your sense of security, safety, and taking care of your basic needs are all driven by your feelings. Even poor choice-making is driven by your feelings. You may decide to end a relationship in a fit of anger, or you may tell your boss what you really think. You may bring harm to someone because of a strong emotional reaction. In all of these cases, your choices were being made by a strong or habitual feeling.

In *Stage One*, you were asked to imagine what you desired. You were encouraged to determine whether what you desired was really a core desire. Once you decided what you wanted – what your core desire was - it was suggested that you hold the vision for what you desire. Finally, you were asked to begin to decide what idea you would take action on by setting your intention.

In *Stage One*, the process we discussed for attracting your hopes, wishes and dreams was based on a mental and spiritual process. I asked you to reflect on the spiritual process of attaining what you desire, determining where ideas come from, and I suggested that they may come from your divinity. But if we only approach our hopes, wishes, and dreams from a mental standpoint, we may find that what we desire is not manifesting in our lives.

How many people have you known who had great ideas but never seemed able to make them manifest? If you only approach your ideas from an intellectual viewpoint, without including the power of strong feelings, it's like trying to drive an automobile with no gasoline in the fuel tank. Feelings are the fuel that ignite our ideas and provide that passion and fire for what we desire.

There has been a great deal of research conducted recently on the power of the heart. The scientists and researchers at one of the premier research facilities in the world, the Institute of Heartmath located in

Boulder Creek, California (www.heartmath.org), have discovered some fascinating facts about the power of our hearts.

Their studies discovered that 60% to 70% of the cells of the heart are actually neural cells identical to those of the brain. This discovery suggests that the heart is the major center of intelligence in human beings. They have also discovered that the heart is the body's most important endocrine gland, exerting a tremendous effect on our immune systems and our tolerance to stress.

Of critical interest to introducing you to *Stage Two* is that the Institute of Heartmath researchers have determined that the heart is 40 to 60 times more powerful than the brain. When the brain and heart are working together – when they are *entrained* - our entire system, including our thoughts and our feelings, are "in sync." Keeping our heart and brain entrained increases the probability that you will be successful in attracting your core desires, hopes, wishes and dreams.

The most powerful emotion in the universe is love, and it would be helpful at this point to think about the people in your life for whom you feel deep love. Where do you feel this love? Not in your head. Not someplace outside of yourself. You feel it in your heart. In *Stage Two*, we will be exploring the power of your feelings and preparing you for the launch of your ideas. Please know that whatever you put your heart into will become manifest in some form in your life.

Now, hopefully, you have begun to realize the power of your divinity and what things are possible for your life and the type of world you envision. When your ideas are infused with the power of love, all things become possible!

ACTION STEP

IN *STAGE ONE*, you were asked to develop your ideal life in eight areas and, through the power of your imagination, to envision what your desired life would be like in each of those areas.

In this stage, I want you to revisit those eight areas:

Spiritual:

Personal:

Financial:

Career:

Family/ Relationship:

Social/ Emotional:

Physical/ Health:

Mental/ Educational:

WITH THESE EIGHT areas in mind, find a quiet spot, settle in and get comfortable, and close your eyes. Then envision a *particular* desire, just as you did in the exercise in *Stage One.* Hold the idea of that that desire in your mind, and then begin to *feel* that desire in the area of your heart. Stay relaxed, but focus and concentrate - really make this process real. With all the feeling and emotion you can conjure up, infuse your desire with feeling, holding these emotions in your heart. I know these steps appear to be repetitive, but this process responds to repetition - I am helping you increase the energy around what you really desire.

If you are having trouble with this exercise, then you may be blocked. You could be blocked from succeeding at this exercise because you do not really want your desire, or it could be that you are simply having a low emotional day. Try the exercise again when you are feeling in a good place emotionally – solid, energetic and confident.

Ideally, you will feel your heart open up, and feel the joy of the anticipation of your desire manifesting. In that flood of emotion, you will know that you have just announced to the universe your intention. Remember: by law, what you send out returns to you. That law made it possible for the universe to be formed, through intention and the power of feeling.

Once you complete this exercise, and know you were successful in it, revisit the other desires you wrote down as core desires. Repeat this exercise with them as well, and watch while your dreams and desires manifest in your life.

Remember – the basic message of *Step Two* is to **feel the feeling**. Welcome to the power of your divinity and your choice-making!

CHAPTER SIX

CONVICTION

"The influence which is most truly valuable is that of mind over mind."

-- Lydia Howard Sigourney

CONVICTION

(n. belief, faith, principle, certainty, confidence, fervor)

THE FIRST BUSINESS transaction I ever entered into was the first step in my lifelong love affair with the Beach Boys. It began in 1963, when I gave a friend in my neighborhood Jan and Dean's single, *Surf City*, and seventy-five cents for The Beach Boys album, *Shut Down, Volume Two*.

That one album was just not enough. I began buying each new Beach Boys' album released. I listened to their albums each and every day, over and over. I was mesmerized by their vocal harmonies, and the creativity the group exhibited in the 60s that reached far beyond the limitations of surf music.

I was so influenced by this group that when they were introduced to transcendental meditation, I immediately went out and enrolled in a class on meditation. To this day, I meditate on a regular basis. Throughout the 60s and 70s, as I went through adolescence and grappled with young adulthood, their music was a refuge for me. My passion for the group and their music led me to an understanding of how a core desire can be manifested by the strong feelings such a desire generates.

To tell you the story, I have to step back a bit. As told in the introduction of my first book, *Remembering Our Spirit*, in 1979, I had a spiritual awakening that led me to make a number of changes in my life. I became very aware of the value of goal setting – at that time, it seemed that everything I wrote down on a piece of paper manifested for me. Emotionally, I was experiencing deep *feelings* of being connected to my spirit, and nothing seemed impossible to me.

I had seen the Beach Boys in concert, and in the early eighties I found myself wanting to see them in concert again. But I had discovered through some research that they had been to San Antonio, the city where I live, just one time, and the concert had been very poorly attended. As a result, the group said they did not want to return to San Antonio.

But I was undeterred. I sat down with a piece of paper and outlined an image for my attendance at a Beach Boys concert *in* San

Antonio. My vision expressed my desire for front row seats at the concert, and in my vision, I not only attended the concert, I met the group as well.

It is important at this stage of the story that you understand that I was still strongly influenced by the spiritual awakening I had in 1979. At that time, I believed (as I believe now) that nothing was impossible!

I took my image into meditation, and I envisioned this musical group coming to San Antonio, and imagined meeting them. I put the image in the drawer of my bedside table and went about the business of my daily affairs.

Then one night, about a month later, I woke up with the strangest feeling. My "little voice" was telling me to call the local concert line that indicated musical groups that were scheduled to come to San Antonio in the near future.

I dialed the concert line and began listening to the various musical acts that were scheduled to come to San Antonio. To my joy, I heard that the Beach Boys had scheduled a concert. I leaped out of bed yelling and screaming and jumping up and down - I was that excited about what was unfolding.

I did not know how long the word had been out about the Beach Boys coming to town, so I didn't know what seats for the concert might still be available. Hoping for the best, I sent in my ticket order for my own ticket, and for tickets for some friends who planned to attend the concert with me.

About two or three weeks later, I received the tickets in the mail. I paused for a moment before I opened the envelope to remind myself not to be disappointed if I did not receive the seats I had envisioned.

When I opened the envelope, my eyes fell on the seat numbers. I had to look at them twice because I could not believe it – I had been given front row seats to the concert! By this time, I was beyond celebrating. I was in awe, astounded by what was transpiring. Everything about my image was unfolding before my eyes.

That left just one desire around this vision: meeting the Beach Boys. How was I going to make this part of my vision manifest? I began meditating on this desire, and after a few days, I hatched an idea and put it into motion. I called the airport, told them that I was doing a story on the Beach Boys, and asked of was there a way to meet them to conduct an interview.

I was told that the musical groups that come to San Antonio did not fly into the main airport. They landed at an auxiliary terminal next to the airport, a facility that afforded them privacy and security from fans like myself! The airport officials also told me that they did not know when the Beach Boys were scheduled to arrive.

A little disheartened, I went to the concert with my friends, and we all enjoyed a great concert from our front row seats. After the concert, I told everyone that I needed to take off, not letting them know that I still *believed* – with all my heart and soul – that I was still destined to meet the Beach Boys.

I drove to the airport and turned onto the road that took me to the nearby terminal where I had been told musical groups generally took off and landed. As I walked up to the terminal, I saw the tail end of a bus that I recognized as being the bus that the Beach Boys had taken to the arena. I ran inside the terminal, wearing my Hawaiian shirt and carrying a book about the Beach Boys that I hoped would soon be filled with their autographs.

Inside, to my dismay, the terminal was empty except for a gentleman sitting at a desk. I ran up to him and asked if the Beach Boys had left yet. He pointed to their plane on the runway and told me that I had better get on board because they were getting ready to take off. I realized that, because of the Hawaiian shirt I was wearing, he thought I was part of the band.

Without hesitating, I ran out onto the runway, toward the ramp that, luckily, was still attached to the plane. Out of breath, I ran up the stairs and into the plane. All of a sudden I was in the middle of a dozen people, some of whom I recognized as the backup musicians in the band. Everyone stopped talking and looked at me with that bewildered look that indicated they were wondering "who the heck is this guy?"

I then noticed one of the Beach Boys, Bruce Johnston, and I stepped up to him and introduced myself. He autographed my book – and shortly thereafter, Mike Love, the lead singer of the group, emerged from a back room of the airplane, and before he went back inside, he signed my book too.

I was told that the Beach Boys were in a private meeting and could not be disturbed. One of the backup musicians mentioned I should leave pretty quickly or I would be going with them to Houston. As you can probably guess, I did have a moment of hesitation in which I thought about staying on the plane – but I was school teaching at the time, and I knew there would be consequences if I stayed on the airplane and did not show up to teach the next day!

So, feeling elated, I departed the plane. I was thrilled that I had met some of the Beach Boys, but, even more, I was in a state of awe at what had just manifested based on a set of goals that I had written on a piece of paper. This experience taught me a great deal about how a core desire can manifest. A few days after the concert, I realized that one of the main reasons my vision had manifested was that I not only had *deep feelings* about my desire for it – I also totally *believed* it would manifest. I had discovered the power of conviction.

CONVICTION COMES FROM a place deep within us. It is faith put into action. Conviction is an unconscious process that does not need validation – we needn't think about it. It is something ingrained in us and it happens naturally when we are focused and in touch with our spirit.

Conviction differs from a core desire, in that a core desire is something you have identified as a dream or vision that you want, deeply. Conviction is the next step in manifestation. It says *not only do I want something, but also I know that something will happen for me.*

The reason I shared the story about the Beach Boys with you was to emphasize the reasons why that goal or image manifested. First, I had a *deep feeling* about what I desired. I realize now that the Beach Boys' music touched an emotional chord in me, and energized my emotions and my desire.

My emotions were also running high because I was still in a heightened state of expectation as a result of my spiritual awakening a few years earlier. I point all of these events out to you to help you to realize the importance of energizing your goals, your wishes and desires with intense feeling.

Secondly – as my story illustrated – I didn't just rely on deep feeling to cause my vision to manifest. I also had the conviction, the belief, that my dream would be made real.

When we approach life with a burning desire flowing from our heart, we are literally magnetizing the very thing we desire to bring that desire into our lives. This is how life works. Nothing is held back from us.

Our challenge is to overcome the illusion that we are victims - that some people are lucky and some people are not. We have to break the illusion that we are sinners and that God has chosen who does and does not deserve to be happy. We are all creatures of the Divine, and we have the ability to create wonderful things in our world if we choose to, and if we believe that is possible to do so.

Conviction helps us manifest what we feel deeply about, and it also helps us when we are faced with challenges. Do you believe this is a friendly universe we live in? Or do you feel like a victim, and believe that God does not care for you? Remember that all is mind, and that what you believe is what you attract in your life. Change your beliefs, and you will change your outcomes.

My convictions are validated when what I envision becomes manifest physically for me. Over the years, I have realized that my goals, hopes, wishes and dreams become manifest because I make a decision *inside* myself to make these things so. Once I understood that everything in my external world first originates inside me, then I knew how to make things happen, and I understood the *source* of my happiness —my connection with my spirit!

ACTION STEP

PART OF BEING able to manifest your hopes, wishes and dreams is to become conscious of how your convictions have guided your life up to this point. Think about your life and, in a journal, write down those major events in your life that have occurred because you decided you *wanted* those things to happen. How did you arrive at the career you are engaged in? Did you ever save money and take a special trip? Did you set a financial goal for something you desired? Did you decide you wanted to get married? Did you want to start a family? In these examples or any others that you can think of, how did conviction play a role in these events transpiring in your life? How important is *conviction* in manifesting your hopes, wishes, and dreams? Where did your convictions come from and why did you desire these things? Do you know what a conviction feels like?

AFFIRMATION

I see Spirit's wisdom in each moment of my life – even in adversity. My spiritual growth often comes in unexpected ways, and provides me with a chance to grow. I approach life with the conviction that I am a divine being, and all that I desire and deserve is now coming into my life.

MY CONVICTIONS AND my core values are intimately bound together. For example, I believe in living my life with integrity. Sometimes that means I must tell people what they do not want to hear. Many times it means saying "no" to situations that I feel are inappropriate. When I honor my core values, I am living my life with conviction. Either a situation contributes to the growth of my soul or it does not. I believe setting boundaries is important in our lives so that we are living our lives with integrity and learning when to say "no" and when to say "yes." Can you identify what some of your strongest convictions are, and what is important in your life? And do your actions honor these convictions on a daily basis?

My Thoughts —

"You have to discover you, what you do, and trust it."

-- Barbara Streisand

I DROVE BY a restaurant today and the billboard outside it read, "Walk by faith, not by sight." What a wonderful message. I find at times that my faith depends too much on what I see, externally. I feel I have to have something manifest to reconfirm my faith – instead of believing (as I should) that my faith is always in Spirit, no matter whether something manifests externally or not. There is so much going on beyond the physical, so much that cannot be realized by my eyes. My "inner eyes" are my true indicator of what is occurring in my world, and those inner eyes are part of my convictions. Conviction is my internal validation. Through it, I find my faith is validated by what occurs outside of me. I am learning that everything outside of me is a reflection of my internal thoughts and beliefs.

My Thoughts —

*"Life only demands from you the strength
you possess."*

-- Dag Hammarskjold

I REALIZED TODAY that everything in my physical world has a spiritual significance. I went to open my front door, and I noticed that I put the wrong key into the lock. This incident made me realize that my desires, and how they manifest, function like keys in a lock. If I don't approach life with the right key, then the doors to what I desire will not open, and what I desire will not become manifest in my life. My "aha" in this moment was to realize that *the presence of certainty of belief opens the pathway for me.* In other words, my convictions are the keys that open the right doors for me and allow life to bring to me what I desire. Today, I wrote down what my convictions about life and myself are so that I was assured that I was carrying the right set of keys for the doors that I wish to open.

My Thoughts —

"They are able because they think they are able."

-- Virgil

WHEN MY BUSINESS is slow or I am trapped by some of my habits, I sometimes whine more than I wish I did; but what I am happy about is that my convictions and my core beliefs are not affected by personality issues and my ego. I truly believe in the power of my spirit, and even though I can become anxious about something or hard on myself, my core belief is that everything will eventually work out, or that my life rhythms will eventually change. When we find our spirits, we know without a doubt that life has a purpose. And even in our most difficult challenges, if we are in touch with our spirit, we know where to go to renew ourselves and remind ourselves of who we are. I have been told many times that we are not given any challenges in life that we do not have the ability to overcome. I believe that challenges are presented to us only as reminders that we must go to our spirit to deal with them.

My Thoughts —

"Experience is hard teacher because she gives the test first, the lesson afterwards."

-- Vernon Law

I WAS REMINDED today of exactly why the goals and images that I set up happen. Once I write down a goal and take whatever actions are appropriate, I let go of the goal and know that Spirit is handling "how" it is going to happen. What I have realized is that letting go of my goals and trusting the process is a validation of my convictions. I truly believe in a higher power that provides for whatever I desire. As a soul, my thoughts, my words and my actions are a signal to Spirit of my intentions, and through the power of choice I have the opportunity to live my life according to my convictions. Everything that occurs in my life is the result of a belief pattern. If I have something occurring in my life that I do not want , then I need to look at my belief patterns. Life is our greatest teacher, and it is our duty to discover the purpose to our lives and then embrace that purpose!

My Thoughts —

"Make it a point to rid your speech and thoughts of all forms of negative self-talk."

-- Author unknown

I HAVE HAD the privilege of being exposed to some examples of spontaneous healings. These healings have occurred in individuals who were pronounced terminal by the medical establishment. I was told that the secret of why these people were able to heal themselves was rooted in their belief system and their convictions. Instead of trying to heal the physical ailment as if it existed, these individuals found a place inside themselves that dealt with the illness as if it never existed. In other words, they saw themselves as being whole and perfect, and the result was the spontaneous healing of their ailment. The power of conviction combined with proper visualization can have enormous implications in our lives. The day will come that we will learn to deal with our problems and illnesses from a place inside of ourselves where the *source* of our wellness resides.

My Thoughts —

"As soon as we learn that God does things through us (not for us), the matter becomes as simple as breathing, as inevitable as sunrise."

-- Agnes Sanford

David D. Dameron

YESTERDAY I DELIVERED a short stress management workshop to adults who work at an elementary school. I don't like to conduct such quick sessions, but I made an exception in this case as a favor to a friend. The challenges are great in these presentations because the people attending do not know me. Additionally, it took place at the end of the teaching day, and the attendees were tired and wanted to go home. But I proceeded as I do in all my presentations, talking to them with the conviction that the information I was presenting was exactly what they need in their lives. I was pleased – though not surprised – by how many people came up to me after my lecture that said they felt like I was accurately describing their lives. They said they appreciated the tips I gave them on reducing their stress. I believe very strongly in my messages to my clients, and today was a nice validation of this fact.

My Thoughts —

"Character is the architecture of the being."

-- Louise Nevelson

ULTIMATELY, I DO not believe we can advance in life and gather experience for our souls without taking risks. Risks can come in a variety of forms, from leaving a job to starting a business, buying something that you really desire, deciding to get married, or telling someone how you really feel. It takes courage to risk, and many times our fears prevent us from taking chances in our lives. But when you truly decide to live your life from your convictions, opportunities and breakthroughs occur that give you the confidence that you are not alone in your decision-making. What is the worst thing that could happen if you decided to live your life with purpose and conviction? If your life has no purpose then living is just a meaningless series of events. I would hope that you contemplate these words, and choose wisely how you will approach life from this day forth!

My Thoughts —

"The secret is this: strength lies solely in tenacity."

-- Louis Pasteur

David D. Dameron

OUR PARENTS, TEACHERS and friends have an enormous influence on our lives. In the case of our parents, they want the best for us, but many times they try to impose their own belief systems on us so that when we are adults, we will see the world as they do. I was reminded of this fact when I saw an episode of the television show *Joan of Arcadia*. In it, the main character was learning to play her own game when she was competing at chess, rather than playing according to the strategy her opponent was imposing. The program reminded me that it's important for me to develop my own belief system, live my life in integrity, and not try to live my life according to someone else's expectations. This understanding does not mean that I don't honor what others believe; it just means I must realize that life is an individual proposition, and I must develop my own set of values and convictions that will best assist in the development of my soul.

My Thoughts —

*"The future belongs to those who believe
in the beauty of their dreams."*

-- Helen Keller

THERE IS A saying that the "identity we live is the identity we experience." Can you imagine what our lives would be like if we chose to look at life the way our creator does? Or maybe in the way that Buddha, Krishna, or Jesus Christ look at life? Think of the conviction behind God creating this universe; consider the higher power's belief that if we were given the power of choice, we would eventually make good choices and live life the way this higher power sees life. Our higher power so loves us that it does not interfere in our choice making. It allows us to experience pain as well as joy. Maybe our potential and the myriad of possibilities for our lives are greater than what we realize! I invite you to consider this possibility from this day forth, and live your life with divine conviction, finally accepting who you really are and what is possible for your life.

My Thoughts —

"What the mind of man can conceive and
believe, the mind of man can achieve."

-- Napoleon Hill

CHAPTER SEVEN

HEART

"To find our calling is to find the intersection between our deep gladness and the world's deep hunger."

-- Frederick Buechner

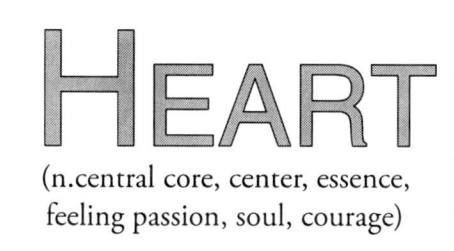

HEART

(n.central core, center, essence, feeling passion, soul, courage)

THERE HAVE BEEN several pivotal points in my life at which events took place that were crucial to my transformation and my spiritual journey. For example, I remember in the summer after my sixth grade year, I made the decision to ask my parents if I could go to a private school in Louisville, Kentucky. That decision was the first in a series of decisions that eventually led to my living in San Antonio, Texas, where I now reside.

Another such defining moment was my spiritual opening in 1979, which I wrote about in my first book. In that moment, I consciously began my spiritual journey to discover who God was and how I could improve my life. A pivotal change occurred in my life in the mid-1980's, when I came to fully understand the power of surrender, as a result of problems I encountered when I tried to start a new company that I really wanted to be successful. I wrote about that realization in the chapter on surrender in my second book.

The transforming events I want to relate to you now occurred in the late 1980s and early 1990s. Like other stories in my life – and, probably, in yours - this story is based on a fork in the road of my life, and the choices I made there. At that time, I was working as vice-president of a marketing company . The money was great, and I had quite a bit of influence in the hiring and direction of the employees of this company.

But then things began to change in my company. The first changes involved senior management, and I realized, looking at the business practices of the new managers, that I was not going to be able to remain with the company. I remember one night lying in bed, unable to sleep. I was in such turmoil about what was going on in the company that I made the decision that night not to wait and let fate take its course, but instead, to resign my position immediately.

In the moment I reached that decision, I felt my heart open up. I knew that I had made the right decision. But though my heart was convinced, my mind was not. It began throwing out obstacles - what was I going to do for work? Why didn't I stay with the company until I found something else? But though my mind made some good points, in the end, the position that my heart took, that I was making the right decision, won out.

After resigning from the company (to everyone's surprise), I began laying out the foundation for a training and consulting business that I had always wanted to start. Attracting new clients was a slow process, and soon I was beginning to suffer some financial hardships as a result of no longer having the income from my previous job, and not yet having my new business up and running.

To compound the issue, I was ending a relationship with a woman whom I had met just after my divorce had been finalized. Although she was a wonderful spirit, I was not happy in the relationship, and that unhappiness was an added stress, in addition to the pressure of my deteriorating financial condition.

Between the monetary strain and the ending of the relationship, I was becoming depressed. My mind was obsessing over what was not happening in my life, and things were looking bleak.

I finally took the courageous step to go into counseling. I found an excellent counselor, and she began to help me sort out my fears, identify my values, and determine what was important to me in how I wanted to live my life. I found just having someone to talk to made me feel better, and helped me begin to learn how to express my emotions.

It was in the midst of all these changes that a crucial change occurred in my life. A friend of mine from the Institute of Heartmath in Boulder Creek, California came to San Antonio to deliver a lecture at a church, and she and I spent some time together one afternoon. I was sharing with her how unhappy I was with my life at this time, the risks I had taken, and how those risks had not yet yielded any new directions for my life.

After listening to me for a while, she responded by saying that she felt that my life was too much under the control of my mind. My fears, worries, and anxieties, she said, were all part of the mind. She began to talk to me about the importance of listening to my heart as well, and keeping my heart open.

She suggested I remember the high points of my life, and keep in mind the memories I had of things events, and people that made me happy. She quizzed me about what activities I was engaged in that kept me in touch with my spirit. Her suggestions began to give me a new outlook on my life. That afternoon, she and I even played frisbee, and by the end of our visit, I felt my heart open up. Such a radical, positive change in my outlook had a strong and palpable effect on me, and suddenly I felt connected to my spirit again.

My change in attitude changed everything connected with my life. Within weeks, I was attracting new clients, and I had successfully launched my new business. I began meeting new women, and my dating life became healthier. I called and thanked my friend for helping me break through these challenges that – though I hadn't realized it - I had created for myself. She gently reminded me to be aware when my mind was in control, and to notice what a difference it made when my heart was in control. She suggested I notice, as well, what was occurring in my external world, and to recognize the difference between how things looked when I chose to be guided solely by my mind, or, conversely, when I chose to follow my heart. I told her that I was determined to choose to follow my heart! And as you might expect, she agreed.

IN SOME OF my workshops, I teach the concept of integration. The term *integration* is used to describe a process under which the suggestions put forth by the mind are considered, and attention is also paid to the heart.

The mind has its uses; it does a great job when analysis and reasoning are called for. Our hearts make a great guide when we wish to forge meaningful relationships in our lives. The research that is being conducted on the power of the heart is quite exciting, but in particular, what I want to point out to you is the role your heart plays in your spiritual development.

I am often asked what it feels like to be in contact with Spirit or God. How do we know if we are really tuned into our spiritual essence? My answer is that when you learn to consciously feel things, be aware of those feelings and recognize what they feel like, then you will have a glimpse into how God operates in your life.

Trust the guidance that comes when you ask for an answer or some direction in your life. If you are feeling anxiety, fear, or worry about a situation, then you are in your head. Your heart, on the other hand, is about joy, peace, and compassion. Your heart is about laughter. When was the last time you felt bad after laughing?

Emotion is our strongest ally in our pursuit for a higher quality of life. Our minds are powerful when we use our imaginations and act on our intentions; but when you add to the mind the power of the heart and the deep-seated feelings about what you desire, then you literally become a magnet for attracting whatever you hope for.

The important point for you to understand here is that following your heart and imagining your dreams are internal processes – they all take place inside of you, though they may manifest outside, in your life. When your desires do finally manifest in your life, they do so because they came from within you. Your heart is the source of your power. This is what author Joseph Campbell meant when he said for us to "follow our bliss."

Jesus talked about the power of our hearts. Buddha spoke of the power of compassion. Our entire universe was birthed out of love, and love is the glue that holds all of creation together. Your heart is your connection to that creative power. When you fall in love, you do not do so in your head. You feel it in your heart.

When our hearts shut down and we become angry and spiteful, why do you think we have heart problems? Is it strictly from eating habits - or do you think that there are other causes for heart problems?

The heart has a wide range of emotions, from joy to sadness. Express your feelings. Have the courage to live your life from your heart. In doing so, you will find your spirit, and when you do, your life will become a direct reflection of this connection.

ACTION STEP

AT THE TOP of a piece of paper, write *Anchor List*. I'd like you to then list five things that, when you think of them, bring you joy or happiness, or make you laugh. Some examples on your list may be a person, a place you have traveled to, your favorite song, your favorite TV episode or scene in a movie, or maybe an event that occurred in your life. As you are recalling these things and writing them down, take a few moments to observe how you feel. You may notice how good you feel by just remembering these things. After you have written down five things, put this list in your purse or wallet so you can carry it with you at all times. Whenever you are feeling anxious or upset about something, take a few minutes, close your eyes, and "anchor" by thinking about one or more of the things you have written down on your anchor list. It is important that you anchor by taking this feeling into your heart area.

In a few moments you will feel better, and you can look back at what was bothering you and decide how you want to handle the situation. Things look different when you approach them from a heart space instead of a head space. Practice this technique often until you can instantaneously transform your feelings around any situation from negative into positive.

AFFIRMATION

I open wide the door to my heart, and I let my love flow out to all of life. I choose to allow God's love to embrace me, guide me and support me.

TODAY, I CONDUCTED a personal consultation with one of my clients who had taken my time management class. After a few minutes, I sensed something was not right with her. In a caring way, I asked her what was really going on with her. She broke down and began to cry, and for the next thirty minutes I just listened as she opened up about some problems she was having. Afterwards, she was so grateful to have had someone to talk to who seemed to care. All I did was listen. I did not say a word. In such situations, I am reminded that listening to someone in a non-judgmental way has more impact than trying to psychoanalyze them. I realized today that listening is about keeping my heart open. I felt very empowered today.

My Thoughts —

"Power is the ability to do good things for others."

-- Brooke Astor

David D. Dameron

I have discovered how my intellect and my heart differ in their impact on me when I am making decisions. I was trying to decide today whether to accept an assignment with a new client. My intellect wanted to make a list of "pros and cons." I went through this mental exercise, but I found myself still in conflict. So I quieted my mind and asked my heart what I wanted, and then the decision became very clear for me. In a flash, I knew that this was not an assignment I really wanted to take on. So I called the prospective client to tell them that I was declining their offer, only to have the telephone ring a few hours later with a new client who had been referred to me. After some discussion, I began to feel that this second opportunity was a much better assignment for me. This event really made me realize that, when I follow my heart, "one door may close, but another will open."

My Thoughts —

"If you care enough for a result, you will almost certainly attain it."

-- William James

A WOMAN WHO is a very close friend to my wife and to me called today to tell us that one of the family's dogs had passed away. I felt great sadness for them. Their dog's passing reminded me of how much I love our dogs, and how hard it will be when they die. I reflected on the realization that loving something has two aspects to it. The joy of loving something is wonderful, but when I do love something and that something passes away, I find myself wondering whether the risk of loving is really worth it, compared to the pain I experience when the object of that love passes on. I am reminded, though, that the joy of loving is far more satisfying than holding back the love I feel for something. People and dogs make their transitions. This is part of life, but I must remember that death is not the last stage. Always choose love, no matter what you fear the future might bring.

My Thoughts —

"If you miss love, you miss life."

-- Leo Buscaglia

THE PAST SEVERAL thousand years have witnessed the birth of hundreds of religions and spiritual groups. Many great spiritual texts have been written regarding the purpose of life and how we should live our lives. But no one, definitive answer seems to have been accepted by all; I am often asked by my clients what is the truth, and is there truly a secret to happiness, joy and abundance? My response is quite simple: Live each moment of your life in love. Think loving thoughts. Speak loving words. In all of your actions, express your love to the world. When you are giving and receiving love, you do so through your heart. You know how this makes you feel and you learn to live your life from this special place. I think sometimes that as human beings we make things harder for ourselves than they have to be.

My Thoughts —

"Nothing is impossible to a willing heart."

-- John Heywood

WHEN YOU FIND yourself feeling unhappy, fearful or anxious, I suggest that you try making a list of things that make your heart feel good. My own list consists of many things that make my heart feel happy. Thinking about my wife and my children fills my heart with joy. Playing with my dogs always brings me joy and happiness. Our backyard is landscaped with colorful flowers and rose bushes, and I always feel at peace when I walk through our yard. Certain memories make my heart sing when I think of them. Sometimes just letting my emotions out and crying about something seems to open up my heart. Calling or doing a kind deed for someone also make my heart feel good. I like the way I feel good about myself and life when my heart is open. I always feel in touch with my spirit when my heart is open – in those times, the voice of my inner guide is clear.

My Thoughts —

"Teach my unskilled mind to sing the feelings of my heart."

-- Anna Young Smith

THERE ARE TWO approaches I practice in order to keep my heart open. One approach is to just engage in life with unconditional love, without judging people for their actions or beliefs. I also try to do caring acts for others, as an important action step to keeping my heart open. The second approach involves avoiding *over care*, which I've found can actually close my heart down. By *over care*, I mean there are times that I have wanted to help people so much that I have interfered with what they are supposed to learn, what their struggles are meant to teach them. I find I am involved in over caring when I interfere without people even inviting me to help them. When I over care, I find myself worrying about a person, and worrying about what they are experiencing . I have to remind myself that every human on this planet is learning how to find their spirit, and I must allow them to do so without imposing myself on them unless I am invited to do so. I can exhibit empathy and caring in situations, but I must remember that people learn through their choice making and actions, and even though their choices are different than mine might be, the lessons they've chosen to learn are theirs to choose, not mine.

My Thoughts —

"In a full heart there is room for everything, and in an empty heart there is room for nothing."

-- Antonio Porchia

THE PURPOSE OF prayer, meditation and visualization is to achieve *feeling* within ourselves. So when you pray, pray with feeling. When you meditate, meditate with feeling. When you visualize, visualize with feeling. Observe what feelings surface, and embrace these feelings in your heart area. Send these feelings to all corners of the universe, and do so knowing how powerful your heart really is. If you embrace these feelings with every ounce of your heart, in this sacred place, you will make contact with your spirit and you will begin to understand how your spirit communicates with you. Your decision-making will change as you "feel" what to do instead of "think" what you need to do. The intellect is important, and useful, in some situations - but once you learn to separate the voice of your spirit from the voice of your ego, your feeling nature never fails you.

My Thoughts —

"In order to create, there must be a dynamic force, and what force is more potent than love?"

-- Igor Stavinsky

WHEN YOU DISCOVER how to love unconditionally, you realize that life is teaching us all of the time. Today, I saw a preview for a movie about the struggles of a man who was mentally challenged. The point of the movie was not what others could teach the man, but rather what he could teach us. By learning to express love, care, and compassion in the world, we find these qualities inside ourselves. Then, instead of judging others, such as the mentally-challenged man in the film, we come to realize the gift that he really brings us. There is an intelligence behind all of creation, and my admiration goes out to the individual who can see spirit and love in great situations as well as in horrific events.

My Thoughts —

"A willing heart adds a feather to the heel."

-- Joanna Braillie

I HEARD GREGG Braden speak today at a conference. He is one of my favorite authors, and a fine public speaker. In his talk today, he spoke of some of the latest research into our DNA structure. He said that our DNA structure responds to our emotions. It begins to respond when we experience feelings such as gratitude, love and compassion. What scientists have discovered is that only a third of our DNA is turned on. The other two-thirds has not yet been activated. Gregg said that the potential for growth and power is huge, if we can learn how to turn on the DNA that is currently turned off. He feels that emotions are the key to turning on these codes. He reminded us today that every emotion has a corresponding chemistry in our bodies.

My Thoughts —

"The only thing that makes one place more attractive to me than another is the quantity of the heart I find in it."

-- Jane Welsh Carlyle

139

IN MY STRESS management workshops, I talk about how our nervous systems are separated into two branches: our sympathetic system and our parasympathetic system. When you are anxious, fearful and overly stressed, your body is in your sympathetic system. Staying too long in this system can have very deleterious effects on a person's health and mental outlook. The key is to keep our bodies in our parasympathetic systems. This system brings balance and enhances our longevity and the quality of our lives. Exercising, meditation, joy and laughter keep us in our parasympathetic system. The importance of keeping our hearts open is a key component to keeping ourselves in this system.

My Thoughts —

"The most powerful agent of growth and transformation is something much more basic than any technique: a change of heart."

-- John Welwood

CHAPTER EIGHT

Inspiration

"A man who truly wants to make the world better should start by improving himself and his attitudes."

-- Fred DeArmond

INSPIRATION

(n. motivation, stimulus, prompting, igniting, idea, vision, insight, spark)

ONE OF THE surest ways we can serve life is to be an example to others by how we live our lives. There are many such individuals whose lives have served as inspirations to all of us. One such individual is sports cyclist, Lance Armstrong.

Lance first gained notoriety in 1991 by winning the U.S. Cycling Championship. Just two years later, he won the U.S. Triple Crown of cycling. In 1999, he won the first of seven consecutive Tour de France titles. Even with all the accomplishments Lance has garnered, his story is much more than the number of races he has won. His story is one of courage and conviction, and one that has inspired many of us to push beyond our challenges.

Born in 1971 in Plano, Texas, Lance was raised predominantly by his mother in the suburbs of Plano. From a very young age, Lance took part in athletics, primarily competing in triathlons. It was during this time that he discovered his passion for life, which was cycling, and he chose to focus all his energy on his chosen sport. Soon a national cycling team took notice and invited Lance to work with them – though at that time, Lance was only a senior in high school.

Lance quickly began to excel in cycling, garnering the many honors we have all heard about. But in October of 1996, Lance would face a challenge far more formidable than the mountains he was used to cycling. He was diagnosed with testicular cancer, which had spread to his brain and lungs. Doctors gave him only a forty percent chance of recovery from this horrible disease.

But Lance, as we have learned, was "wired" in a different way than most of us. He had a deep desire to live, and that attitude, combined with successful surgery and chemotherapy, delivered to Lance a clean bill of health in February of 1997. His doctors and his many fans were amazed. When asked about his astounding recovery, Lance replied, "It's ironic. I used to ride my bike to make a living. Now I just want to live so I can ride."

Lance Armstrong will always be known for his athletic prowess, but he has also inspired us all by founding various charitable organizations. His determination, his talent and his philanthropy have given him that stature of a true role model. His courage and his story are embedded in our American culture, and he stands as a true example of what the human spirit can overcome. He has endured failure and obstacles in his life, but he never quit.

Often, in interviews, Lance has indicated that he is very goal-driven, and he believes that attaining goals fuel his self-drive and motivation. This inner drive has given him the stamina to overcome a life-threatening disease, and, through hard and persistent work, to become the premier cyclist in the world. Lance Armstrong is the epitome of inspiration.

WE ALL HAVE heroes in our lives, individuals who inspire us by their actions and their words. Inspiration comes from within us and when we become inspired by someone, this is only a mirror of what is occurring inside of ourselves. We are all interconnected, so when someone does something that benefits the world, we all benefit from that deed.

In our journey together in this book, we arrive at another gate in our exploration to attract our hopes, wishes and dreams. Gate Number One was in *Stage One* with *Intention* as we were taught to prepare to take our mental imaging into our feeling natures. *Inspiration* is Gate Number Two, in which we are now preparing to put our ideas into action, which will be covered in *Stage Three*.

Just as our bodies need water and nourishment to provide energy for us to conduct our daily affairs, we also need inspiration. You could imagine that if you stopped eating or drinking water, your physical body would soon shut down, affecting not only your health but your mental and emotional processes as well. Inspiration works in the same way in our lives. Without inspiration, we do not have the fuel to meet our life challenges. Inspiration feeds our spirit, keeping our spirit available to us so we can draw upon it to fuel our lives.

Daily I see the impact lack of inspiration has on lives. I see people who have given up hope; they move through their days like zombies, with no sense of purpose. And yet other people I know approach life with a fierce passion, motivated and inspired by how they live their lives, just as they inspire and motivate others.

Inspiration manifests in our lives when we find our spirit. We become models for others by our words and our deeds, and when we find that place where our spirit resides, we are in touch with a voice that guides us when our life challenges become formidable. Fortunately, we are surrounded by remarkable souls such as Lance Armstrong to inspire us and show us what is possible!

ACTION STEP

IN YOUR JOURNAL or on a piece of paper, write down three people who have been inspirations to you. After each person's name, write a few short sentences explaining what it is about these people that has inspired you. How have these people helped you in your own life? What have these people taught you about yourself, and how have they influenced your beliefs about life?

AFFIRMATION

*There are no ordinary events in my life.
Everything I experience is important, and
is intimately connected to my unfolding
story and my divine purpose. I am inspired
by how I choose to live my life.*

RECENTLY, I HAD a book signing for my second book, and I thought I recognized a woman at the signing – I vaguely remembered seeing her somewhere before. When she came up to me to have her book signed, she said she was a counselor and had heard me speak at a conference a couple of years before, where I had been the keynote speaker. The conference was for school and private counselors, and I remembered my presentation vividly because I could tell that my subject matter was really engaging the audience. At the book signing, the woman said she had been very inspired by my message that day, and wanted me to know how much she appreciated the "tips" I had given in my presentation for reducing stress and living a higher quality of life. I thanked her, and I was reminded that my work and my messages to people could have a positive affect. Who in your life has been inspired by how you have chosen to live your life?

My Thoughts —

"Make the most of yourself, for that is all there is of you."

-- Ralph Waldo Emerson

I WRITE OFTEN of the understanding that how we choose to live our lives can serve as an inspiration to others. When you are inspired someone else's life, that inspiration serves as a mirror for how you may desire to change and live your own life. I was reminded of this fact when one of my friends told me one day that he had started to write a book because he was so inspired by the books I had written. My own actions brought out what was already inside my friend, and was waiting to manifest. I am so grateful to my friend as he reminded me the importance of living my life to the fullest, bringing out my gifts, and allowing my actions to serve and touch others. All acts of kindness, whether large or small, do have the potential to bring change to others and to the world.

My Thoughts —

"I don't want to get to the end of my life and find that I just lived the length of it. I want to have lived the width of it as well."

-- Diane Ackerman

IN ANY GIVEN moment, we make choices that eventually lead to an outcome. We can choose to align ourselves with our life's purpose by doing something generous for someone, or we can, instead, choose to bring harm to someone. By the law of cause and effect, either choice will yield a possible outcome for us. When you are living an inspired life, you will make more positive choices because you feel joy in impacting people's lives in a constructive way. Inspiration comes from your spirit and it is part of your feeling nature. Those who live their lives with inspiration do so from their hearts, for the heart is the gateway to our spirits. Are you living an inspired life? If not, what can you do to rediscover the connection with your spirit?

My Thoughts —

"Whoever loves much, does much."

--Thomas a Kempis

LIVING YOUR LIFE based on inspiration is like jumping into a swimming pool. Until you jump in, you cannot receive the benefits of what you desire. How many times in our lives have we looked at a situation as if we are a detached observer, wanting to make change but afraid to? To benefit from inspiration, you must be willing to abandon the mental states that are filled with fear; you must be willing to *risk* in order to create change in your life. You are a part of the very force that created the entire universe. You are not alone in your challenges. When you are willing to take the risk and make the leap, then you will discover the fire of inspiration. Inspiration does not come from thinking - it comes from doing. And each time you risk, your inspiration will continue to grow. Are you willing to risk? Are you willing to face your fears? Are you willing to claim your divinity?

My Thoughts —

"The greatest happiness is to transform one's feelings into actions."

-- Germaine de Stael

WHY IS INSPIRATION so important in your life? Remember that I have said that *your outer world is a reflection of your inner world.* This means your beliefs, your thoughts, your words, and your actions all contribute to what you are attracting to yourself on a daily basis. You develop patterns of habit, and these patterns do not always contribute to your highest good. Living an inspired life changes those patterns. Inspiration is like a laser that cuts through the toughest areas inside ourselves; it is powered by the knowledge that we know our lives work better when we are in touch with our spirit. What actions and activities could help you find inspiration in your life? How does it feel to live an inspired life?

My Thoughts —

"I used to want the words, 'she tried' on my tombstone. Now I want 'she did it'."

-- Katherine Dunbar

I FIND MYSELF inspired by many authors who are living today. I would really enjoy sitting down with these individuals to listen to their life stories and share ideas and viewpoints. Some of the living authors I would most like to meet are Dr. Wayne Dyer, Dr. Deepak Chopra, Gregg Braden, Richard Bach, and Dan Brown, to name a few. I am grateful to any individual who is willing to put his or her ideas into print and write about subjects designed to help improve the quality of life on this planet. What people inspire you, and why?

My Thoughts —

"To know the real worth of yourself is to
be able to recognize the worth of others."

-- Author Unknown

I HAVE A great respect for social activists and for the great service they often provide to our society. I believe many of us have fallen asleep in allowing our politicians and military leaders to institute policies that are not always been in the best interest of everyone. In my own country, we have great social problems, educational challenges and environmental threats. Activists who stand up for these issues to make us aware that we are facing credible challenges are to be commended for having the courage to speak from their convictions, and warn us. With power, control and greed at work in all areas of our lives, we need to be vigilant of what is happening and be willing to voice our opinions until we are all working together for the greater good of our society and not our individual interests.

My Thoughts —

"If you expect someone else to guide you, you'll be lost."

-- James Earl Jones

HAVE YOU CONSIDERED where your inspiration comes from? Think about the great masters: Michelangelo, Darwin, da Vinci, Aristotle, or Mother Theresa, to name a few. Where did their inspiration come from? When Jesus said, "I and the Father are one," he gave us an insight as to the source of his own inspiration. Could it be possible that we are all drawing upon the same source for our inspiration? If so, can you then realize that there is a solution to every one of your problems? Do you understand that you are not facing any challenge that has not been faced before, by others? If you are willing to consider that you are a divine being, then it would behoove you to find ways to keep yourself inspired and begin creating the world that you desire and deserve!

My Thoughts —

"Life itself is the proper binge."

-- Julia Child

I REALIZED TODAY that I had not been writing in my journal lately. I sometimes feel I do not have anything to write about – that nothing is happening in my life that is out of the ordinary, and worth reflecting on. The reality is that in these periods of my life when my life doesn't seem vital, I am out of connection with my spirit. God does not take days off, and in reality each moment is precious. There are opportunities concealed in each moment of my life, and to act as though there is nothing happening out of the ordinary is just lazy thinking on my part. When one lives an inspired life, each moment has meaning and significance. I know this for a fact, because when I practice my spiritual routines and stay creative, ordinary moments become extraordinary because I am paying attention.

My Thoughts —

"It's the time of your life - live!"

-- William Saroyan

I AM SO thankful that, over the years, I kept all of my journals. I also have several file folders filled with articles, emails, and inspirational notes that I kept, knowing that one day they would become part of the books I intended to publish. Rereading my journals and the inspirational pieces I've kept, there are things that touch my heart. They inspire me, and I hold onto these pieces of information to help me find my way when I am feeling depressed or sluggish about my life. I was once told by one of my spiritual teachers that everything talks to us. Spirit takes advantage of many avenues to deliver its messages to us, and remind us about the possibilities for our lives. Our job is to pay attention. When we do recognize a message of hope being given to us, it can be very inspirational - and inspiration is the fuel that keeps us moving through the many ups and downs of our lives.

My Thoughts —

"You must learn day by day, year by year,
to broaden your horizon."

-- Ethel Barrymore

STAGE THREE

DESIGN THE BLUEPRINT

"Successful people succeed because they know where they want to go. You must decide what you want to be and what you want to accomplish. The best way is to set goals that will point you in the right direction. Goals will also help you to determine when you arrived - or if you have gotten off the track."

-- Soundview Editorial Staff
"SKILLS FOR SUCCESS"

BLUEPRINT

(n.strategy, design, outline, idea, course, agenda, intention)

IN THIS STAGE, you will be taking your idea or your hope, wish, or dream and putting it into a structure that allows your idea to manifest. How important is this process to the fruition of your hopes, wishes, and dreams? Imagine if you were an architect and tried to build a house by just verbalizing your ideas to a contractor. There would be miscommunications, mistaken interpretations of ideas, and no sense of what steps needed to be lined out first in order to accomplish your plan.

Another way to illustrate how important it is to bring structure to your desires is to tell you the story of two wallpaper hangers. Wallpaper Hanger #1 came to his job with some supplies, without having seen the project first. He started working and realized he needed some materials so he drove to the local hardware store. Upon returning, he kept working, and came to realize he needed more wallpaper. So he drove back to the store. All day long he continued to stop work when he realized that he needed some item he did not have, and had to go back to the store. After Wallpaper Hanger #1 had been on the job a couple of days, the customer was beginning to get irritated over how long the job was taking.

When Wallpaper Hanger #2 was ready to start her job, she first spent some time with the customer. Then she measured the area and determined what materials she would need to complete the job. She made one trip the store to buy her materials and, in just one day, completed the same kind of job that Wallpaper Hanger #1 was doing.

This story illustrates how important it is to plan properly. Doing so is beneficial to the scope of the job you want to complete. Writing down the goal of the project and the actions necessary to complete it saves time and money and allows absolute clarity as to the end result.

There is an old cliché that says we need to "work smarter, not harder." The Bible, on the other hand, contradicts this cliché by telling us to work "by the sweat of the brow." I am here to say to you that we can either continue working hard at the expense of our health and our relationships, or we can begin to look at *how* things really happen in our lives. Perhaps it is time to reassess our priorities and be open to looking at different ways to achieve our hopes, wishes and dreams.

Not everything in your life has to be supported by a pre-conceived structure, but for the big projects and ideas in your life, structure and planning can be quite beneficial. In this chapter on *Stage Three,* you will be shown the value of setting goals, keeping your focus on what you want to achieve, and approaching your goals with enthusiasm.

This stage encompasses the action steps that you should take to manifest your idea. As with a garden, planning is not enough. After developing your plan, you must take the action step and plant the plants, water and feed them, and keep the weeds out. Gardening is a wonderful metaphor for how we should approach our plan, and the action steps that follow. We must put the plan into action, keeping our thoughts positive and focused and not allowing any negative thoughts to become like weeds in a garden.

The secret to success at this stage is to understand the physics behind your ideas. Energy follows thought – as I have said, your concentrated thoughts and words, whether negative or positive, become crystallized by an unknown process that leads to creation. This is one of the mysteries of life - that what we think and act on becomes manifest.

By writing your ideas down after you have envisioned them (*Stage One*) and having energized your ideas through your feeling nature (*Stage Two*), you are now ready to bring a non-physical idea into physical reality. You are the conduit. You are the bridge that, through proper action steps, will bring your idea from the realm of thought into manifestation.

When you truly believe in your ideas, believe in the power to make them manifest, and act according to your plan, nothing is withheld from you. Life – your life - awaits the changes brought about by your hopes, wishes, and dreams. And with the grace of God, you become a co-creator, partnering with the very force that created the entire universe from an idea in its consciousness.

ACTION STEP

IN *STAGE ONE* and *Stage Two*, you were asked to develop ideas in eight areas called *Life Impact Areas*. These areas were:

Spiritual:

Personal:

Financial:

Career:

Family/ Relationship:

Social/ Emotional:

Physical/ Health:

Mental/ Educational:

IN *STAGE THREE*, you are going to work with a powerful tool to help you focus and define your desire. Turn to the Appendix section of this book and refer to the goal sheet you find there. Copy the steps outlined on the goal sheet onto a piece of paper, and then choose one area that represents your desire, and, with it in mind, fill out the Goal Sheet.

The steps on the Goal Sheet include defining your *Goal Statement*. For example, your Goal Statement might be, "I desire to take an Alaskan Cruise with my wife in two years." The next step is to consider *What Obstacles* you might need to overcome in order to reach this goal. In the example of the cruise, saving enough money, or finding a reliable house and pet sitter might be possible obstacles.

Then ask yourself *Who Else* needs to be involved in this goal. It could be a family member, your boss or a friend. The next item to consider is *Defining the Necessary Action Steps*. In the case of the cruise, you might call a travel agent and have some cruise catalogs sent to you. Once you choose your cruise, you might need to call the agent to begin completing the necessary paperwork. You might then book your travel arrangements, and choose your shore excursions. As you get closer to leaving for the cruise, you will need to take care of stopping your mail, getting traveler's checks, and buying any needed clothes. The specifics may seem endless, but taking care of them makes it possible to enjoy your cruise.

In this step *Step Three*, it will be important to list the *Start Date* and the *End Date* for each action item over the next two years. Doing so is part of making a good plan, so that you won't neglect any necessary details or feel rushed as your trip approaches.

Next, as part of this *Step Three* process, you identify the *Reward*, or payoff for accomplishing your goal. Relaxation, intimate time with your partner, and a time of utter indulgence and relaxation for having worked hard at your job are some possible rewards.

The final step is to consider what your *Next Goal* will be, the goal you take on once you've accomplish this one. Listing your next goal keeps you proactive and focused on bringing the things into your life that add enjoyment and purpose to your existence.

CHAPTER NINE

Goals

"I never have to grope for methods. The method is revealed at the moment I am inspired to create something new."

-- George Washington Carver

ONE OF MY closest friends is Mikail Davenport, whom I have known since 1980. I owned a bookstore in the early eighties, and I eventually sold it to Mikail. This wonderful soul has been such an important part of my life, and in the last few years, he has become such an inspiration to me and for many others.

I asked Mikail to write me his story as I felt his joys and challenges would be inspiring to others and would emphasize how important it is to set goals, and what we can attain when we do so.

Mikail sent me the following letter, and I have inserted it in this chapter just as it was sent to me. His story is one of the triumph of the human spirit, and its power to overcome unbelievable challenges.

He writes, "My life had an ignominious beginning. Upon hearing he had a son after siring two girls nine and ten years earlier, my father demanded that the hospital staff remove my diaper to prove to him my gender was accurate!"

"The next eighteen months were uneventful, until New Year's Day, 1950, when I was struck with polio in an epidemic that paralyzed or killed over fifteen hundred children. Fortunately, my polio was only paralytic, not bulbar, so time spent in an 'iron lung,' the 1950s euphemism for a respirator, was minimal. I have vague recollections of being in a ward of hundreds of crying children. It was so short-staffed that the nurses had to put the trays of food in the cribs for those of us who could feed ourselves and let us wallow about, like pigs at the trough. I place no blame here, but just to recount a horrible recollection of being paralyzed and unable to eat, short of sucking food off a tray."

"The doctors told my mother that the best thing she could do was to put me in a 'home' as I would never walk again nor be very functional. She promptly told them where they could stuff their diagnosis and embarked on a crusade to get me back on my feet. For the majority of my childhood, she would drive me back and forth from San Antonio to Galveston, Texas where I spent three months or more of every year undergoing reconstructive surgery and painful rehabilitation."

"By kindergarten, I was able to walk with forearm crutches and a long-leg steel brace. The crutches went away about two years later. By high school, I was quite adept at walking with the brace and was able to participate in most high school activities, including a high ranking on the swim team. By college, I was walking unaided, with only a slight limp. I am eternally grateful to my mother for her uncompromising courage, hope, and stalwart faith in God's ability to heal and care for His\ Her children."

"Life went on pretty well until I hit my early thirties. Increasing daily pain levels and muscular weakness in my left leg brought me back into a leg brace. I was diagnosed with post-poliomyelitis syndrome, the recurrence of polio symptoms, and a prognosis of eventual muscular failure once again."

"By this time, my mother had made her transition, and I was facing the prospect of being crippled again and all alone. My faith at that time was at its lowest ebb, and my anger towards God became greater and greater."

"The next ten years brought further disability, but I began to resign myself to the fact that I was heading downhill physically, and that I had to do something to buoy myself above the raging sea of anger and despair that came and went as frequently as the waves of pain and periods of collapse."

"I took up Tai Chi Chuan to strengthen what muscles I had left until I could no longer stand for more than fifteen minutes at a time. I began a program of spiritual seeking and eventually found a path that brought me closer to my creator and greater peace within myself. I bought a wheelchair and decided that I would move onto the next stage of disability with resignation and strength of will."

"At age 51, I began working out with a personal trainer, who to this day is the person I honor and credit with moving me into the field of optimum health, regardless of my disability level. With each workout, I began to feel more alive, more centered, and more able to face my disability's challenges head-on. At 53, I answered an advertisement seeking physically challenged individuals to form a wheelchair track team. Intrigued, I dove into this adventure and took to it like a fish to water. I won my first five-kilometer race in 2001 and became addicted to inner power, strength, and wholeness that athletic accomplishment brought me. I entered and finished third in my first marathon using my handcycle in 2002."

"Soon after, I was diagnosed with lung cancer, and I had a malignant tumor removed. That experience was the most spiritually enriching periods I had had up to that time. Instead of anger, I felt joy to have discovered it early. Instead of fear, I embraced it yet as another challenge to overcome. Instead of being worried about recurrence, I focused on getting myself back in shape for another race."

"Eleven months later, I triumphed and took third in my second marathon. Four months later, I finished a six-day, two hundred and thirty-two mile race through Alaska, the longest wheelchair and handcycle race in the world. I am now preparing for yet another marathon, it being the third since my bout with cancer."

"While in the hospital recuperating from cancer, I asked God to direct me where I should go next. His\ Her answer became clear when I returned from Alaska. I founded an organization whose sole function is to support and provide resources for physically challenged people in their quest for physical, mental, and spiritual health to the maximum of their level of disability. My motto, and the name of the organization is, 'Disabled, Not Unable."

"I consider my original polio as the greatest blessing in my life, as it made me aware of the pain and suffering so many other people endure, not just physically, but emotionally as well. I know in my heart of hearts that it has made me a compassionate and better human being. My cancer brought on its own set of rewards and enabled me to push myself. It gave me a window into how adversity, when handled appropriately, can produce healing at many levels and in ways unfathomable at the time one is going through it."

"I could have done with a lot less suffering, but I try to say, 'Hey God, it's me, Mikail. What next?' I am waiting, ready to welcome whatever it is because I know it's for my own healing!"

WHEN I ASKED Mikail to write a condensed version of his life with polio and cancer, the one area that he emphasized repeatedly to me was the power of setting goals. The reason I wanted to use his story in this chapter was because I know that physical activities have been almost impossible for Mikail since he was in his thirties. Working out had never been a priority for him.

Through the grace of his medical challenges, he began setting goals, and the result has been phenomenal in terms of what he has accomplished. What was not included in his story is the number of people that Mikail has touched and inspired with his accomplishments. He has brought public awareness and deepening acceptance to those who are handicapped, and he has made the public more aware of the needs of the physically challenged.

The power of setting goals can have phenomenal effects in our lives. Our thoughts, words and actions are extremely powerful, and when we focus our energy in a direction of our choosing, our intentions are often accomplished.

The subtlety of goal-setting is that we can accomplish our goals two ways. We can impose our will and, through hard work, make things happen. Or we can relax and let Spirit pave the way for what we desire. Our culture leads us to take the first approach most often. We have been brought up to believe that working hard is the pathway to results, so I believe we are intimately connected to this intelligence. What I would have you consider in the second example is that there is another way to approach achieving our goals – by approaching life with "God's will" rather than by approaching it with our own will.

The point of this book is to suggest to you that perhaps there is an intelligence that knows what is best for us and knows how best to bring about what we need. Once that intelligence shows us what to do, then it does become our responsibility to make the effort to take the action steps. In order to trust in a higher power, you have to have conviction, faith and patience.

ACTION STEP

In *Stage Three,* you were asked to fill out the ***Goal Sheet*** that is located in the Appendix of this book. You were asked to pick one area and one goal for that area that represented something you really desire. Now that you have filled out your goal sheet, you are ready to launch you idea. In this *Action Step,* you are being given the guidelines to launch your idea - but before doing so, I suggest that you read the rest of this book with special attention to *Stage Four.*

Here are the guidelines for launching your goal:

1. Sit down in a quiet space at a time when you are in a positive and peaceful frame of mind.

2. Close your eyes, take in several deep breaths, and clear your mind.

3. Envision your goal as if it is completed. See it. Feel it in your heart. Rejoice in the manifestation of your goal.

4. Let your vision go and affirm its completion for your highest good.

5. Begin your action steps.

6. Keep yourself organized, motivated, and pay attention!

AFFIRMATION

I have a clear idea of what I desire in my life. I willingly follow my inner direction, and I do so knowing that whatever I desire is manifesting in my life.

I ONCE HEARD a story the actor Jim Carrey recounted about his days prior to becoming a well-known movie star. He had decided to go to Hollywood and try to get some auditions for parts. Carrey found that, like many actors who are first starting out, his rise to stardom did not occur overnight. In the story he told, Carrey recalled sitting in his car overlooking Hollywood, wondering about his future and thinking about how very much he desired to be a successful actor. He pulled out his checkbook and wrote a check to himself for $10 million and he dated the check for three years in the future. He then put the check into his wallet. Three years later - on the exact date that he had dated the check – Carrey was given his first major role, for a fee of $10 million, exactly the amount for which he had written the check. This amazing story is a testimony to Jim Carrey's core desire, his intention, and to his commitment to a goal in which he believed.

My Thoughts —

"In order to succeed we must first believe we can."

-- Michael Korda

MANY YEARS AGO I set my intentions and goals for my business. One of those goals was that my revenue should exceed my expenses. That goal represents a principle that I believe in deeply. I have never believed in incurring debt, and I've realized over the years that the concept of being debt-free is a core value that I believe in. For the last fifteen years, and since I started my business, I have attained that goal - my revenue has always exceeded my expenses. I believe I've been able to attain this goal because, first, I believe that Spirit is the source of my abundance. Second, I feel that I respect money and where it truly comes from, so I handle my finances in a very pragmatic way. Third, I have great appreciation and gratitude for my prosperity.

My Thoughts —

"Always plan with the end result in mind…Be clear. Be specific."

-- Stephanie Goddard Davidson

MY GOALS KEEP me focused. Often, when my life is not going the way I want it to, I realize that I have become lazy in my thinking and, more importantly, lethargic in my daily routines. Goals keep me on track whether it is with my walking program, a target weight goal, or staying on schedule with writing my next book or developing a workshop. Some people are more disciplined than I am - for example, some have no problem regularly working out. Exercising is not my favorite thing to do, so to make sure I exercise regularly, I have to set goals, such as walking three or four days a week. If I don't set goals, then I easily fall into lazy patterns. When I do set goals, and keep them, I feel better about myself, and I feel in better connection with my spirit.

My Thoughts —

"Men's natures are alike; it is their habits that carry them apart."

-- Confucius

My DAYS SOMETIMES feel like an endless "to do" list, with more to do than it seems there is time to do it. I am a creative person, and as a result, I can easily get too many projects going at once. I need to revisit my goals from time to time and prioritize by deciding what it is really important for me to accomplish at this time. By letting go of unimportant things and being more realistic about what projects I can get done, I allow space for new opportunities and ideas to come in. I approach projects as though my life were a glass of water that I try to only fill halfway. If it is only filled halfway, I have room for more water if I need it. If I am always overfilling my glass, then I am usually not accomplishing something so much as creating a mess that I have to clean up!

My Thoughts —

"As you wander on through life,
sister\brother, whatever be your goal,
keep your eye upon the donut,
and not upon the hole."

-- Sign on a coffee shop in Chicago

MY MAIN GOAL in life is to learn how to be in constant communion with my spirit. I believe that being in connection with my spirit and listening to my inner guidance contributes to my feeling that my life has a purpose. I believe that the quality of my life, my health, my relationships, and my abundance are all directly connected to my main goal. I have set a very lofty goal for myself, but my goal is ambitious because I am tired of my ego and aspects of my personality that I've allowed to create disruption in my life. I prefer letting Spirit guide me. The challenge is to stay in the presence of Spirit on a moment-by-moment basis.

My Thoughts —

"Set your course. The important thing is where you want to go from here."

-- Author Unknown

I HEARD THE host of the television reality show *Survivor* make an important point about the importance of goals. He told some of the contestants to "set a goal first and then harness your energy." He was referring to the fact that one of the teams competing on the show was not performing well because the people on the team were acting as individuals, instead of working together. His observation was that the team they were competing against was working better and expending much less energy because the team members had agreed to common team goals. I thought this was a great example of how goals give our lives direction. It illustrated that goals help us to focus our energy, rather than scattering our energy in too many directions because we have no clear intention.

My Thoughts —

"In the long run we only hit what we aim at."

-- Henry David Thoreau

TODAY MY GOAL was to *live* each moment of my day, seeing life as I would see it through the eyes of my spirit. I made a conscious effort to listen for direction, each moment. Should I eat or should I wait? What should I eat? Which route should I take to my appointment? Throughout the day, whenever my thoughts started to wander, I took time to center myself. The result was an unbelievable day. Time seemed to disappear. I looked people in the eyes, being very present for them. My connections with people and situations felt very different. And I began to understand the difference between looking at the world through my physical eyes and looking at it through my spiritual eyes. I like this goal; I'm thinking I should make it my permanent goal!

My Thoughts —

"Action is eloquence."

-- Shakespeare

AT THIS STAGE in my life, I am approaching goal-setting with a completely different focus. I am taking my goal into my daily meditation and asking Spirit to bless my goal, and show me how to move toward it. Then I am turning my goal over to Spirit, and putting my attention on what actions I should take to assist the goal coming into creation. One my goals is that my books become known, and successful, on an international scale. Instead of jumping into the standard marketing role, I have asked Spirit to assist me with attaining this goal. I am excited at the potential Spirit will bring to this goal, and anxious to see what transpires as I have a deep desire to manifest things in my life from the inside out!

My Thoughts —

"In creating, the only hard thing is to begin."

-- James Russell Lowell

I AM AMAZED at the success of three of my new workshops, *Adventures in Self Management, Advanced Techniques* and *Master Training*. These workshops were not only fun to create, but have also been amazingly well-attended. I exceeded all the goals I set for these classes, and I realize their success is the result of my having turned the marketing of these classes over to Spirit. In my younger days, I would have felt the need to knock on doors to get people to take a look at my classes. But once I turned the matter over to Spirit, I found people calling me out of the blue, or responding to a notice I had sent to them, without any kind of follow-up on my part. So today, I am practicing Internal Marketing. My initial results are exciting, and each day I become more grateful to this mysterious and loving spirit that runs the entire universe, and who is waiting for my command.

My Thoughts —

"You always miss 100 percent of the shots you don't take."

-- Author Unknown

TODAY, ONE OF my clients told me something that really touched my heart. She had just taken my *Beyond Time Management* workshop, and had begun to use an organizer that I had given her at the workshop. She said the organizer had become "the walking stick of her journey." When I asked her what she meant by this statement, she said that she was now writing goals down in her organizer, and that she was making sure that her "to do" list was representative of the priorities in her life. She was happier in her job, she felt her marriage improving, and she was consciously creating more time for activities that would enrich her spiritual life. I was happy for her, and thankful to Spirit for guiding this person to me so that I could be of service to her. She also served me, by giving me feedback that lets me know I am achieving the goals I've set for my business.

My Thoughts —

"The end of life is life. Life is action, the use of one's powers. And to use them to their height is our joy and duty."

-- Author Unknown

CHAPTER TEN

Focus

"The greatest successful people of the world have used their imaginations...they think ahead and create their mental picture, and then go to work materializing that picture in all its details, filling in here, adding a little there, altering this a bit and that a bit, but steadily building — steadily building."

-- Robert Collier

FOCUS

(n.center, pinpoint, direct, fix, sharpen, concentrate, home in on)

ONE OF MY clients, a schoolteacher, told me about an experience he had that taught him a lesson he's never forgotten. Before he became a schoolteacher, he was a manager for a restaurant chain. Each week the district manager for the restaurant chain would come to my client's restaurant, and they would do a "walk through," making sure the restaurant was up to the standards set by the home office.

On one trip, the district manager and my client went outside to inspect the garbage bin. When they opened the bin, they were surprised to see several pieces of silverware. It was obvious that someone working at the restaurant had not wanted to clean the silverware, so he or she had just thrown it away.

The district manager looked at my client and told him that he wanted this matter cleaned up right away, and my client replied that he would take care of it. But on his next inspection, the district manager and my client looked in the dumpster and found silverware in the garbage once again.

"Why have you not taken care of this situation, as I asked you to?" the district manager asked. My client responded that he had not had time, but that he would get something done about the issue right away. However, what followed shows that a second promise to get something done was not enough.

The district manager looked at my client and said, "I'll take care of this matter myself, right now. Because you are fired." The district manager said he was firing my client for two reasons – first, because he felt my client did not know how to set priorities and see them through. Secondly, he felt my client too easily lost his focus, and was unable to juggle several things at once – a necessary quality in a restaurant manager.

My client told me that getting fired over this issue changed his life. He realized that he had become unfocused, that he had lost his ability to set priorities, and that he had somehow lost his desire to

185

do an outstanding job. Every day revolved around crisis management because he had lost his focus.

To MANIFEST YOUR hopes, wishes and dreams, it is critical that you keep your focus. When we become unfocused, our energy becomes scattered. We make mistakes, forget things, and we wear ourselves out trying to handle the challenges we've allowed our lack of focus to create.

But when we are focused on our intentions, we align ourselves with the universe, and the universe cooperates with us. We pay attention to our thoughts and our words, and we act with great care and attention. Living in the Information Age, as we do, the high volume of information that reaches us each day, from many different sources, challenges us to remain focused.

You will know when you are starting to lose your focus by the problems you encounter. It may take you twice as long to perform tasks. You may notice you've begun to bump into things because your mind is going in a thousand different directions. You might find yourself having near misses when driving your automobile. And you will almost certainly have trouble concentrating when someone is taking to you.

To return to a state of focus, work on becoming present and totally in the moment. Become utterly focused on the task that in front of you, as though you were using a magnifying glass to fully experience the issue that glass is trained on. Focus your thoughts, and keep them positive. Keep a "to do" list, and keep up with it, rather than relying on your memory.

Finally, live each of your days from your heart, being fully present and focusing on the pure enjoyment of life, whatever you are doing. Our sacred connection to joy is heightened when we are in connection with our spirit. When we are focused and working in collaboration with our spirit, then everything we desire and hope for is brought into our lives. All physical manifestations are nothing more than focused energy!

ACTION STEP

ON A PIECE on paper, list the hours of the day from the time you rise (such as 6:00 a.m., 7:00 a.m., etc.) to the time that you normally go to bed. Next, think about any and all the activities you could engage in that would make you feel connected to your spirit and energize you, and assign that activity a time. For example, if walking or going to the gym helps connect you to your spirit and energize you, what time of the day are you going to do this activity? Do you have a hobby or a sport that you would like to engage in today? If so, choose the time span that you will schedule to work on that hobby or sport. What about how you start your day? Do you set aside some quiet time before you go to work? Do you have something inspirational you could read? How about setting a time for a period of meditation or prayer? Do you want to set aside time for your family or your friends today? Remember to consider and identify your priorities.

Make time for the things that are important in your life. Set goals and write them down, every day. Soon this exercise will become a habit, and you will feel good about yourself because you are getting the things that matter most to you done, and taking care of your spirit!

AFFIRMATION

I speak, think and act positively, and the universe responds in kind. I refuse to indulge in negative emotions and thoughts, and I focus only on what I want created in my life.

I NEED TO remind myself each day of the benefits of meditation, prayer, and creative visualization. Doing so helps me control my mental pictures and my internal dialogue, and that keeps me in tune with my spirit and my ability to attract what I truly desire. My life is a reflection of what I put my attention on, and I am finding that on a daily basis I am challenged by how my mind wanders in many different directions. I lose focus in these moments, and I feel out of connection with my spirit. I desire to be focused on the present moment - looking for the good in life and listening to my spirit.

My Thoughts —

"Go placidly amid the noise and the haste, and remember what peace there may be in silence."

-- Desiderata

WHAT SEPARATES THOSE individuals who seem to manifest a high quality of life – what makes the difference for them? What makes one person prosperous and another person poor? Why does someone attract a wonderful life partner and another feels like they will be alone the rest of their lives? The secret to manifesting our hopes, wishes, and dreams lies in *focusing* on what we desire. That means getting up each day and living your life as if what you desire *has already happened.* It also means seeing your life as if it is already complete. Staying focused means holding the vision for the thing you desire each day until your desire manifests physically. Remember that energy follows thought, and that our entire physical universe was created by an idea in somebody's consciousness. So do you create your own world, each and every day!

My Thoughts —

"The present time has one advantage over every other — it is our own."

-- Charles Colton

ONE OF THE main challenges in life is to realize we are each conditioned from birth to look at things in a certain way – and that conditioning may limit what we are capable of. We are influenced by our parents, friends, and teachers. We are influenced by what we read in the newspaper, what we hear on a radio, or what we watch on the television. All of these influences cause us to develop habit patterns, and we make our choices from these patterns. The quality of our lives is a reflection of the choices we make. Therein lies our challenge. Do our habit patterns enrich our lives or do they hinder us? To change deep-seated patterns that limit us takes self-discipline and focus – but the rewards are great. What patterns do I want to change in myself, and what actions will I take to change these patterns?

My Thoughts —

"Those who wait till evening for sunrise . . .
will find that they have lost the day."

-- Elizabeth Hamilton

WHY IS STRUCTURE important in our lives? Because structure gives us focus. I am not talking about a rigid approach, where you plan out each and every moment of your life. I am talking about how you control information that comes in, and control how you approach each day. We all have daily responsibilities that are part of our duty to our families, our friends, and ourselves. But we can get so caught up in the mundane – in running around doing our errands and other duties - that we lose our focus and forget about the important things that really contribute to the quality of our lives. Think of *structure* as a *focused vision*. What do you really envision for your life, and what is the real source of your abundance? Are your thoughts focused on the real source of your abundance and happiness?

My Thoughts —

"*Real generosity towards the future lies in giving all to the present.*"

-- Albert Camus

FROM TIME TO time, I realize I am finding it difficult to be positive in my words, my thoughts and my actions. I realize how my tendency to be judgmental and critical has subtly crept into my daily life and comments. For example, I notice that I'm regularly complaining about such small matters as my irritation that the weathermen cannot seem to forecast the weather accurately. I notice how cynical I have become of our politicians, and of my tendency to be critical of all politicians. Then I make an effort to change that attitude. I want my focus to be on what is the best in people, rather than getting caught up in their personalities and egos. I am discovering how easy it is to be critical, and I do not like that in myself – so I resolve to change.

My Thoughts —

"Press on: nothing in this world can take the place of perseverance."

-- Calvin Coolidge

David D. Dameron

YESTERDAY, AS I was driving to an appointment in San Antonio, I found I had a number of unrelated thoughts running through my mind. Suddenly I found myself in a part of town that was unfamiliar to me. I had taken a wrong turn off the expressway – something that rarely happens to me. I tried to correct my mistake, and became frustrated when I kept taking wrong turns because I was not familiar with the area of town, and was unable to get back to the expressway and continue to my appointment – and my time was running out. I was going to be late, and, in the midst of trying to correct my error, I realized how unfocused I was. I do not like how I handled this situation. It gently reminded me of my need to work to remain present and focused on the moment.

My Thoughts —

"The future never just happened. It was created."

-- Author Unknown

TODAY SOMETHING REALLY embarrassing happened to me that made me determined to get more focus in my life. I recently joined a new gym, and this morning I went to work out. I was unfamiliar with the layout of the gym, but wanted to enjoy the sauna after I had walked the treadmill and found it. Before entering the sauna, I removed my glasses, and I cannot see well without them. While in the sauna, I realized I needed to go to the bathroom, so I walked out of the sauna without my glasses on and went into what I thought was the men's restroom. When I could not find a urinal, I realized that I wasn't in the men's restroom at all, but was instead in the women's dressing room. Since I was in there anyway, I used the restroom, and on my way out, bumped into several women walking out of the shower. They were stunned to see me, but I just kept walking. As I opened the door, there were several men in the hot tub watching this whole event, and they started laughing at me. I felt I'd had enough of a workout, got my glasses and my things and walked out of the gym, thinking life was letting me know that I clearly needed to get more focused.

My Thoughts —

"Life is now in session. Are you present?"

-- B. Copeland

I AM STARTING to realize I've taken on a great deal in my work, and that leads to a lack of focus. It's difficult to keep my mind on task - I find myself starting to obsess over how much I have do to get ready for several workshops that are coming up. I find myself becoming impatient when people do not call me back with information I need to conduct these workshops. My mind is on too many things at once. As I see myself starting to lose focus, I find that I have to return my focus to the moment, and follow the plan I have laid out. I remind myself that things will get done if I stay focused, and that worrying about things over which I have no control over only creates more challenges.

My Thoughts —

"Do what you can, with what you have, where you are."

-- David Sarnoff

TODAY I AM taking a workshop about an ancient healing method called Reiki. I do not have the opportunity to take workshops as often as I like, but I have several friends who have become Reiki Healers, and who feel that their lives have been enriched by learning this healing method. What I discovered in the workshop, to my enjoyment, was how focused and in the moment I am when I am practicing Reiki. I felt in connection with my spirit and, to my delight, my ability to focus didn't just benefit me - the people I worked on using this method actually felt better. Reiki forces me to focus my energy and my concentration, and I am learning the benefits of such focus in all areas of my life.

My Thoughts —

"*This is what binds all people and all creation together — the gratuity of the gift of being.*"

-- Matthew Fox

197

YEARS AGO I became interested in the ancient art of dowsing. I was intrigued by the ability to locate water or other things using dowsing rods. As I did more research into this subject, I discovered the secret of dowsing. Great dowsers use focus and concentration when engaging in this practice. They hold a vision for what they are seeking; that focus registers in their nervous system when they come across the subject of their focus. The impulse then registers in their fingers and the dowsing rod reacts to the impulse. Recent research shows that a dowser's brain waves react positively to their being able to focus and concentrate. The important point here is not whether one believes dowsing is effective, or not. The point is the power of focus and concentration, and what those qualities can bring to our own lives.

My Thoughts —

"Nobody can conceive or imagine all the wonders there are unseen and unseeable in the world."

-- Francis P. Church

CHAPTER ELEVEN

ENTHUSIASM

"Through some strange and powerful principle of 'mental chemistry' which has never been divulged, nature wraps up in the impulse of strong desire, 'that something' which recognizes no such word as 'impossible,' and accepts no such reality as failure."

-- Napoleon Hill

ENTHUSIASM

(n. eagerness, keenness, feeling, fervor, zeal, passion, interest, spirit)

I HAVE LEARNED over the years that there are no accidents in life. Every moment is filled with purpose, and I was reminded of this truth one day. I was on my way to consult with a client, and was traveling down a highway in the city of San Antonio, where I live. As I was driving, a car pulled up beside me and the driver began waving at me wildly. My first thought was that I must have done something to cause the driver to respond with road rage.

He motioned for me to roll down my window and when I did, he told me that my right rear tire was going flat. I thanked him and, as I slowed down in preparation for exiting the freeway to check out the tire, I noticed my steering wheel had begun to vibrate from the effect of the flat.

I pulled over to the side of the road and changed the tire, all the while reflecting that there had been a lesson here for me. I had not been paying attention. I had been preoccupied by thoughts about my upcoming meeting, and as a result had put myself in danger, and had put other drivers in danger as well.

I arrived at my client's home a bit late and began to consult with him on various issues, still keenly aware of the lesson I had just learned: that it's important to remain aware and alert to the unexpected and the subtle clues that are just beneath the surface of ordinary consciousness.

My client was saying that he was struggling with all the details of his work and was wondering why he could not seem to reduce the paperwork on his desk. He was hoping I could give him some guidelines on ways he could make better use of his time. But as I listened to him, I realized that the first step in helping him had nothing to do with time management methods or paper management tips.

My senses having already been alerted by the incident with my flat tire, I was listening to him, but also paying attention to what he was NOT saying. Instinctively, I told him that he had lost his sense of purpose in his work, and that his lack of enthusiasm was the cause of his lack of focus.

I shared with him stories of several of my clients who also had very demanding jobs that involved large quantities of paper, but who seemed to glide through their paperwork, all their tasks easily accomplished. What I had discovered in working with these clients was that they had connected their "to-do lists" with the belief that their work had meaning. And in finding meaning in their work, they had also found enthusiasm that inspired them to focus on their work, and do it well.

These individuals felt an almost divine connection to the many details of their daily lives. They worked with purpose. They exhibited an unbridled enthusiasm. When my client heard their stories, and the connection to meaning, it struck a chord with him and he said he realized what he needed to do was to reconnect with his life's work — the work that, for him, most held a sense of purpose.

The problem identified, my client and I both thought that our consultation was over, but we were wrong. The divine had something else in mind for us. My client suggested we drive my car down to the corner tire shop to get my tired repaired while he and I continued to talk. He followed me in his car and waited for me on the street while I handled the details with the mechanic. As I walked outside, I saw my client talking to an elderly man at the end of the street. This man was standing next to his bicycle, which had two paint cans hooked onto the back.

As we drove back to my client's house to finish our meeting, my client told me a bit about his conversation with the elderly man. The man had said that he rode his bicycle around town all day painting over the graffiti on the walls of the businesses in the area. He had been doing this for years and felt that it was his contribution to the community. In fact, the city of San Antonio was so impressed with this man's mission that they began furnishing the paint he needed.

My client remarked about how inspired he was with enthusiasm with which the elderly man approached his work. Whether it was cold or hot outside, this man did not detour from his intention. It was clear to my client and to me that, through this elderly man, we had been shown someone who had discovered his purpose in life. And by finding his purpose, he had chosen to approach life with enthusiasm, and the community on the south side of San Antonio was the beneficiary of his enthusiasm.

How MANY OF us can get up every day and say we understand the purpose of our lives? How many of us are continually inspired and enthusiastic about our lives and our daily routines? Your own work may not involve painting over graffiti; it may not even involve public service. But what matters is that your work is something that you feel is important, for whatever reason — that you feel your work has purpose. And when you find your purpose, there you will discover enthusiasm.

Please understand that enthusiasm is a choice and is a reflection of what is occurring inside of you. Its existence is rooted in the element of *fire*. And fire is a direct reflection of our energy level. To live a life of quality and meaning, we need fire to get through our daily affairs with enthusiasm. Keeping our energy level high and finding purpose in *everything* we do is what unleashes the power of fire within us, and the enthusiasm that follows.

When you discover your connection to Spirit, then you approach life with a different attitude. You make different choices. You enter into an intimate relationship with your own life, and you'll find that everyone you come in contact with looks to you for ways to raise their spirits. People are drawn to you like a magnet because your enthusiasm inspires them. They want to know how you found that inner connection. You become a lighthouse, not just finding your own way, but also showing them the way on their own journey.

Enthusiasm brings us to *Gate Number Three* as we prepare to enter the final stage of the manifestation of your hopes, wishes and dreams. With your imagined desires and with your feeling nature ignited, you now enter *Stage Four* and participate in the creation of your world.

ACTION STEP

THINK OF THE most influential spiritual person in your life. Don't hold back. And don't limit yourself - You may feel that it is the very divine force – Jesus, Buddha, or a patron saint, for example – that influences you most. Whether the person you choose is religious, spiritual, or metaphysical, you are going to create an amazing and intimate experience between yourself and your choice. Here's how. Tomorrow, from the moment you get up, I want you to take on the personality of the person you have chosen. Go through your day with only one focus: seeing the world as the person you chose would see it. In other words, your task will be to *see the world through this person's eyes*. Treat people as this person would treat people. Think *only* the kind of thoughts that you imagine this person would have. At the end of the day, write down your experience in your journal. How did you feel about the experience? What difficulties did you encounter in trying to stay focused? How did people react to you? Mastering this technique actually gives us a glimpse into how we should live our lives on a moment-by-moment basis. We are divines beings, aspects of the very force that created this universe. To embrace our spiritual origins is to claim our real power and live our lives with enthusiasm.

AFFIRMATION

What I desire in life must be a reflection of the actions I take. My life is a mirror of my choices, and, in each moment, I choose to live my life with unbridled enthusiasm and love.

ENTHUSIASM COMES FROM the Greek word *enthous,* which means literally to be in God, or to be possessed by God. In Greek times, people were said to be *enthous* when they had a certain look in their eyes, or they spoke in very confidant and loving way. They had a certain smile on their faces, and people were drawn to them because they had a certain energy and charisma about them. What excites you and brings forth your passion? Are you aware of the *source* of your enthusiasm? Are you living an inspired life filled with purpose and motivation? Are you *enthous?*

My Thoughts —

"My grandfather always said that living is like licking honey off a thorn."

-- Louis Adamic

Today I had an epiphany. I was watching actor Tom Cruise being interviewed by talk show host Oprah Winfrey. Tom has just entered into a new relationship with a young woman, and he was not shy about telling everyone on the show how much he was in love. As the interview progressed, it became apparent that Tom Cruise is very genuine about the quality of his relationship with those he meets in his life. His enthusiasm for life was a nice reminder of how I have recently allowed my energy level and positive approach to life and my thoughts to drop, and that I needed to get reconnected to life and remember what my purpose is. Since that interview, I have felt myself in a better place, and I thank Tom for being a reminder of how we can serve others by how we live our lives.

My Thoughts —

"Live all you can; it's a mistake not to."

-- Henry James

David D. Dameron

I HAVE FOUND that there is a direct connection between the level of my enthusiasm and how I feel about my life. What I have discovered is that when I am following my heart – my *bliss*, as Joseph Campbell puts it - I feel more enthusiastic. When I am teaching or helping people, I feel very connected to my spirit. I feel my energy level rise, and the little irritations of life do not seem to bother me as much. It is when I lose my focus and fall into old, limiting patterns of behavior that my enthusiasm for life wanes. I am reminded in these times that I cannot live an enthusiastic and inspired life if I am not in connection with my spirit. So when I realize that I am out of connection, I purposefully engage in activities and daily routines that help me reconnect. I just like how life feels when I am in connection with my spirit.

My Thoughts —

"The greatest of all miracles is to be alive."

-- Thich Nhat Hanh

I RECENTLY REVIEWED all my journals from the past twenty years. I recommend that you keep a journal because it is a reminder of how you are living your life, what lessons you are learning, and how you overcame obstacles that you yourself had attracted. I also look for repeated behavior patterns when I review my journals. Today, I discovered that my journal had many entries bemoaning that nothing was happening in my life. I had written of how my business was slow, or that I was concerned I had not been doing my spiritual routines with regularity. In those entries, I noted that my energy level was low, and I was feeling disconnected from my spirit. What I learned from re-reading those entries today is where I should place my priority in my daily routines. All my activities should reflect my focus on my spirit, and I should make sure to engage in activities that keep me in connection with spirit. Like most people, I have a lot of lazy habits and patterns that I can allow myself to fall into; when I do, my enthusiasm for life is diminished, so it's well worth my effort to remain positive, focused and active.

My Thoughts —

"After a certain number of years, our falls become our biographies."

-- Cynthia Ozick

David D. Dameron

LIFE IS LIKE a mirror constantly reflecting back to us the things we need to look at. A friend of mine who is in the midst of a life transition called me today. During our conversation I reminded him to claim his power, as he was feeling powerless in his challenge. I reminded him to keep his effectiveness up, and his attitude positive, by doing things that energized him. I suggested several techniques, but in the process of working with him, I realized that he was a reflection of my own struggles, and the advice I was giving him reflected things I myself should be doing. He thanked me for helping him, but what I told him was how much he had helped me!

My Thoughts —

"All the significant battles are waged within the self."

-- Sheldon Kopp

WE ALL SERVE each other by the way we choose to live our lives. Since we are all connected in our life journeys in one way or another, what we find most distasteful in someone else is often the very thing we need to look at in ourselves. I was reminded of this fact when I thought about an old boss of mine with whom I'd had much conflict. I disliked his leadership style, yet I had to acknowledge his enthusiasm gave him an unbelievable magnetism. In remembering him, I came to the realization that I was jealous of his enthusiasm – I wished I had more of that kind of energy myself. When I turned from looking at him and his life to looking inside myself, I saw the truth in the saying that we can't control others - the only thing we can control in our lives is how we *are* living our lives. I found that, when I began to change on the inside and embrace a more enthusiastic attitude, my relationship and attitude toward my boss changed as well.

My Thoughts —

"The world belongs to the energetic."

-- Ralph Waldo Emerson

I HAVE A friend who serves as a wonderful inspiration to me. I have known her for many years, and I have observed her rise in life from very humble beginnings. Many obstacles were placed in her way as she moved toward her goal of becoming a Chiropractic Practitioner, and she overcame them all. She possesses a number of great characteristics, but the one admire most in her is her incredible enthusiasm for life. She will always give you a loving smile and laugh with you about almost anything. She is a person who has found her spirit, and her connection with it is obvious in all her interactions with people. I sometimes wonder where she gets the endless energy she exudes, but I know where her enthusiasm comes from. I am thankful for the people in my life who remind me of what my life can become if I, too, keep in contact with my spirit. Do you know anyone who inspires you with their enthusiastic behavior?

My Thoughts —

"To exist is to change; to change is to mature; to mature is to create oneself endlessly."

-- Henri Bergson

WHEN I MEDITATE I find I'm constantly reminded of one particular aspect of enthusiasm: *playfulness*. Play brings balance to my day, and I know I need to play more when I find myself caught up in the "to do's" of life. Playfulness is directly related to my inner child, the aspect of myself that holds my curious, laughing, creative side. I was the prankster growing up in my family, and I was very mischievous when I was a school teacher years ago, and getting in touch with that aspect of myself really fuels my enthusiasm. What kinds of things do you like to do for fun?

My Thoughts —

"Just think: I came to this party to be with my friends. Imagine my disappointment when you showed up!"

-- Groucho Marx

THIS WEEK HAS been devoted to taking better care of myself. I have been meditating, exercising, and reading more. I have spent the week playing in the yard and having more fun. Today the telephone has been ringing all day with clients calling to book workshops with me. My book publisher called and said they were ahead of schedule on my next book. When I reflected on the increase in activity around me, I realized that my energy level was high this week because I had taken better care of myself. And since energy follows thought, I am merely attracting what I am putting out. This week – my energy level, and the results I've seen - has really fueled my enthusiasm, and I feel very connected to my spirit.

My Thoughts —

"Life was meant to be lived, and curiosity must be kept alive. One must never, for whatever reason, turn his back on life."

-- Eleanor Roosevelt

SCIENCE HAS DISCOVERED that our thoughts and attitudes affect the quality of chemicals produced in our brains. Researches know that different parts of the brain are activated by a person's moods. We've come to understand how our immune system can be positively or negatively affected by our thoughts. Living our lives filled with enthusiasm can heighten our quality of life in so many ways; thinking and speaking positively can only benefit us. The key to understanding how to find this positive energy and approach inside yourself is to *find your spirit*. When you touch your spirit, I assure you that you will know it. Your life will be transformed because you will begin to live your life from the inside out, and you will be less influenced by what is going on outside of yourself.

My Thoughts —

"When enthusiasm is driven by confidence, any goal can be attained."

-- Robert E. Regent

STAGE FOUR

Participate in the Outcome

"I do not know what I may appear to the world, but to myself I seem to have been only like a boy playing on the seashore, and diverting myself now and then finding a smoother pebble or a prettier shell than ordinary, whilst the great ocean of truth lay all undiscovered before me."

-- Sir Isaac Newton

OUTCOME

(n. result, consequence, aftermath, end, payoff, effect, wake)

How DO WE achieve our goals? Where do we find ideas to help us with our daily challenges? What separates those individuals who are prosperous from those who are not? Some people attribute their success in life to the quality of education they received. Others might say they accomplished the good things in their life through hard work.

If we read the many self-help books and spiritual texts that fill the shelves of bookstores, we are told again and again that a positive attitude and a belief in a higher power are the ways we can attract what we want in our lives. And if one examines how people live their lives, there is evidence that supports the theory that hard work, education, religion, and even luck, if you believe in good fortune, have been the reason things have happened in our lives.

But in this stage of our journey through this book, I am going to suggest a new *paradigm* to you, a new possibility for you to consider. A paradigm is a framework that contains all the components of our experience together and creates a unified picture of reality - a world view. What makes up a paradigm is relative and subjective, and thereby purely personal, with absolutely no connection to or test in what we call reality.

The key to developing a new paradigm is to understand that in order to change a major paradigm, we must first examine our definition of what is possible. Throughout this book, I have suggested that what you create in your life is directly connected to your thoughts, feelings and actions. We live in a subjective universe; that means that life is impersonal. Life only responds, without judgment, to what we ask of it.

The paradigm shift that I am asking you to consider will challenge thousands of years of human conditioning on how we should judge and value our lives. The evolution of the human race has been about *control*. Our parents told us how to look at life. Teachers instructed us how life operates. Churches told us to look to books and

219

teachers for guidance. Governments asked us to trust them to decide what we needed, and trust them to provide it.

If you look at all these forces that have shaped our lives, you'll see that they have been external forces. If we have been living our lives in fear - fear of terrorists, fear of upsetting our religious leaders, fear of what our parents and friends might think of our actions - then we have in many cases turned our power of choice over to others, to someone outside of ourselves, as though we could trust others to guide and protect us.

The paradigm shift I am urging you to make is this: *I am asking you to claim your power of choice.* I am asking you to consider that you are an aspect of the very power that created the universe. I am asking you to ponder the possibility that everything you could possibly need has been already provided for you, and that by finding your source, you can bring into physical reality anything you desire.

This is not a willful process, but more of an invitation. I invite you to hold your focus and intention, feel what you desire with great feeling, and then, taking the proper action steps, bring into life anything you desire. Life is impersonal. It does not say one person should be rich and another poor. It does not think of you as a sinner. It just is! It exists through us, and us through it.

Like a seed needs water, sun, and nutrients in the soil, life needs us in order to express itself. And life can express itself in a positive way or a negative way – that is what I meant when I said that life is impersonal. If you choose to believe that you cannot be prosperous, then life supports you in that disbelief. If you believe life offers infinite possibility, then life brings you the riches of the universe.

We need to be willing participants in this process. We need to "participate in the outcome." We do this by following the stages I have outlined to you in this book, but we also do a couple of other things. First, we *pay attention* when we launch our desires. We pay attention as life begins to speak to us through other people, books, movies and other sources to show us that what we have asked is coming into manifestation. Everything talks to us if we have the "eyes to see" and the "ears to hear." Secondly, we must express our gratitude for life on a daily basis, thanking life for the riches that will be bestowed in our lives. In doing so, we are giving thanks to that which has already been given!

Focused thoughts infused with great feeling bring us into harmony with the power of our spirits, allowing all of our hopes, wishes and dreams come true. But we have to *believe* such abundance is possible. You have to be disciplined to hold your focus until that hope, wish or dream becomes a reality in your life. And the key point to this book is that the process of manifesting our hopes, wishes and dreams is initially an inside process. We go inside first to forge our idea that will manifest in the outer world.

If you can imagine it, it is possible. And not only is it possible - it already exists, or you could not imagine it. Out greatest scientists and inventors will tell you that through persistent imagining and focus, their greatest challenges were eventually answered.

We can choose to work "by the sweat of the brow," or we can relax and let Spirit bring our desires into manifestation. And since we are spirit, the possibilities are endless for us if we can just break our past conditioning, and old habit patterns.

Finally, look closely at the word "outcome." If you put a hyphen in the word, it becomes out-come. Where is it "out coming" from? All things come from Source. Everything. And since we are an intimate part of this source, then each of us is creating our world, every moment. What does your world look like? Do you believe that you deserve only the best?

In this stage, you get to participate in the outcome of your idea. Much like watching a play or a movie, you get to see the results of your focused intentions. Let your choices be filled with love. May you choose to live the highest possible quality of life. May you make choices that lift the lives of the people around you. May you become a lighthouse, guiding others to what is possible in their lives. May you finally claim and accept your divinity!

ACTION STEP

EVERYTHING IN OUR physical world was originally an idea. Everything has meaning if we are paying attention. In this action step, take an hour and go for a walk outside. You could choose to walk in nature, or downtown in your city. Take a journal with you, and for one hour pay attention to everything you see. Keep your intention – what you desire – in the forefront of your thoughts. If your walk takes you into areas that are natural, what insects or animals do you see? What flowers do you see? If in a crowded setting, what do you hear people saying? What do the street signs say? If there is a flyer on the ground, pick it up to see what it says. Then, after an hour, sit down and journal about what you saw, and see if anything you saw or heard or read had some connections to your intention, your desire, or the goals you have developed through this book. Go to a bookstore and look for books that explain the symbolism of insects and animals. Remember this action step when you read Chapter Twelve, as you will then better understand how *synchronicity* plays a part in our lives.

CHAPTER TWELVE

SYNCHRONICITY

"The secret to success is to be ready when your opportunity comes."

-- Benjamin Disraeli

SYNCHRONICITY

(n. opportunity, opening, in sync, parallel, simultaneousness, coexistence)

In the early 1990s, I made a huge decision to leave my corporate position in a marketing company and start my own training and consulting business. Although there is more to this story, just realize that, for me, this was a huge decision for many reasons especially from a financial standpoint.

I had really agonized over the decision, but something inside me kept encouraging me to take this risk, so I finally resigned my position. The next few months were very uncertain – even more so than I had feared. Starting a new business was more complex than I had imagined. As I watched as my financial situation deteriorate very quickly, I began to have serious doubts about my decision to start this new venture.

It wasn't all bad - I was slowly picking up one or two new clients. But my revenue was far below what I needed to attract to make it. In response, I spent many nights in my apartment having some serious talks with my spirit. On one level, I knew that leaving my previous company had been a good decision. And I reminded myself that I had always wanted to start my own business. I had good reasons, internally, for having made the decision I'd made, but, as yet, my external world was not validating what I felt inside.

Each night, as I meditated on this situation, I kept getting the message to be patient and just pay attention. But another part of me was extremely insecure about the pace at which things were happening, and that part urged me to question whether the voice of my spirit was being realistic about the situation.

But I told myself to have faith. Even in the midst of all my insecurities, I was determined to "stay the course," whatever the cost. I was determined because I believed, at a very deep level, in what I was doing and what I felt guided to do. I also knew that I had no other choice but to follow my heart. This was about more than my financial well-being. My whole approach to spirituality was at stake. I believed the universe would respond to my intention. If it did not, everything

I believed in spiritually was false, and I knew I would end up on the streets with the homeless.

What I did not realize at that time was that, when I made the decision to continue on at whatever cost, I had set in motion a series of events that would once and for all ensure the success my new venture. The pivotal event occurred a few weeks after I made the decision to continue, despite my fears.

I was traveling to a small town in southeast Texas to work with a company that was, at that time, my only client. The company had responded well to my workshops and consulting, so each month I traveled to their location to offer them my services. My usual routine was to consult with the clients in the morning and afternoon, eating lunch each afternoon at the Holiday Inn.

Little did I know what would transpire on one very special day that seemed like a normal day to me. I went to the Holiday Inn for lunch and, to my dismay, when I went into the restaurant, every table except one was filled.

I had only a short time to eat before making an afternoon appointment with my client, so I rushed through the buffet line. I was glad to see the single empty table was still available. I had started eating when a woman walked up to me and asked, "Is that your purse?"

Perplexed, I looked up and responded, "I'm sorry. What did you say?"

The woman asked again, "Is that your purse?" She then pulled the chair out from the table to show that there was a purse in the chair.

I then realized that she had put her purse in the chair to reserve the table while she went through the buffet line. Apologizing, I stood up and started gathering my things, but she said that I could join her as there were still no empty tables in the restaurant. I thanked her and sat down again, and, once she settled in as well, we began talking.

She asked me what I did for a living. I answered that I was a consultant to a local company and was doing some time management training with some of the employees. At that, her eyes lit up. She told me that she worked for the local school district and they had decided that very morning to search for someone to offer time management training to their principals, teachers and staff.

She gave me the name of a person I could call at the district office. We talked a while longer as we finished eating, and I thanked her for allowing me to sit with her. I then went out to my car and immediately called her contact. He was so excited to hear from me that he wanted to see me that afternoon. He said he had a great deal of respect for my lunch companion, and said that if she had referred me, she must have been impressed with my business credentials.

And on that chance encounter, I connected to what was to become one of my largest clients. The school district hired me, and was instrumental in launching my training and consulting business. Thanks to them my business took off, and not long after I secured them as a client, my reputation got around and I was being referred to several other companies. I still enjoy remembering that the success of my business was due to a "chance" meeting at a hotel in South Texas.

FROM ONE PERSPECTIVE, the meeting with the woman at the Holiday Inn's lunch buffet was a random chance event that led to some good fortune for me and my new business. But as you know if you've read any of my other books, I do not believe in chance or "good luck." Every event that occurs in our lives has a cause, and that cause is rooted in our choice-making and our attitude. When mysterious things happen that we can't explain – chance meetings, or timely telephone calls - these events fall into the category of what are called *synchronistic events.*

Synchronicity can be defined as the bridge that joins two events that are connected through their meaning, a link that many times cannot be necessarily explained purely by cause and effect. Psychologist Carl Jung conducted considerable research on synchronicity and came up with three important conclusions.

First, he concluded that there is a connection between mental content (a thought or feeling) and an outer event. Second, he found that, often, individuals can have a dream or a vision that coincides with an event taking place at some distant place, and that the connection is verified at a later time. Third, an individual can have a dream, a vision, or a premonition about something that is going to happen in the future, and their image does occur.

Jung theorized that a synchronistic occurrence was a chain of events that are intimately meaningful to the person who experiences the events. These events may be inexplicable for a standpoint of logic, and, often, are not repeatable. For that reason, you may share with someone an unusual coincidence you experienced, and find the other person dismisses it as mere luck – while to you, the event was intensely personal.

I believe that such an event marks an intimate experience with your spirit. Every event in our life is being orchestrated in relationship with our divinity. When you envision an idea for something you desire and when you infuse that idea with feeling and act on it, it is spirit that causes that idea to manifest.

Our systems of living take a narrower view. In theology, the cause of everything is God. In science, everything is the result of energy. In psychology, everything is related to the mind. Depending upon your point of view, we either live in God or we live in energy – regardless of which approach you support, everything you think, say or act on becomes a process of attracting the very energy and thought you are sending out.

The magic of synchronicity is that *we get to be the willing beneficiaries of our intentions.* Through synchronicity, people come into lives and events occur as a result of our intentions. We cannot always explain these events and occurrences, but life seems to know – even better than we ourselves do - what we need and how to bring our desires into manifestation. To use synchronicity to our best advantage, we have to become willing participants and pay attention in each moment to bring into creation our hopes, wishes, and dreams.

ACTION STEP

IN THIS ACTION step, you will be shown how to recognize the hand of synchronicity working in your life. First, choose a significant area of your life, such as a job you are currently working in, or your relationship with your spouse or significant other. If you are not married or dating anyone, then focus on the city where you live. Now journal on your relationship to your job, a person, or your city. For example, using the job you are working in, take your journal and begin to write down when you started working in your job. How did you find out about the job? Who told you, or how was someone else told about the job? How did you get chosen for the job? How did you get to the town where you found the job? If you follow what I am asking you to do, I'm betting you'll see there was a pattern to you getting the job. During the course of you getting the job, did things happen that appeared to be "lucky"?

You can repeat this exercise using as your subject your job, your spouse, the city you lived in, or any event in your life. What I'm hoping you discover is that your own choices and attitude had a bigger part than you might have realized in finding you your job. Was synchronicity involved in you getting the job? If "luck" does not exist, then how do you explain the many factors that resulted in your success?

AFFIRMATION

I pay attention in each moment to divine guidance as I attract my hopes, wishes and dreams. As I open my heart and mind to the mysteries of life, God's plan for me is revealed, and I embrace my divinity.

OVER THE YEARS certain numbers have come to have significance to me. One of those numbers is 22, and various combinations of 22. It seems that when I am in need of something or I am waiting for something to manifest, the number 22 appears. This number has had significance to me since birth, as I was born on October 22nd. Recently, I was asked to teach a continuing education class for a local school district on the subject of "Finding your Purpose in Life." I agreed to teach the class, but then I began to have doubts. I was ready to back out of the class when I was told it would be held in Room 122. I asked how many people had signed up for the class, and was told 22 had signed up. Because of my history of positive results with anything involving the number 22, I decided to conduct the class after all, and it turned out to be magical. A number of participants told me how fortunate it was that they signed up for the class. Synchronicity works in wondrous ways.

My Thoughts —

*"It is astonishing how short a time it takes
for very wonderful things to happen."*

-- Francis Burnett

I WAS WATCHING an ad on television for an upcoming Disney movie called "Finding Nemo." I sat up suddenly in my chair when the ad showed a submarine marked with the number 22. The very next day, while thumbing through a magazine, I noticed an ad for this movie and saw a picture of the same submarine with the number 22 on it. Based on my history with the number 22, I went out and rented the movie right away. The themes in the movie had a powerful impact on me, as they were messages appropriate for some of the challenges I was experiencing. Some of the movie's themes were "Change yourself, change your world," "When you feel down, keep swimming," and "It's time to let go, everything is going to be all right." I am amazed at synchronistic events. If we pay attention, life is trying to communicate with us all of the time. We just need to learn to recognize the ways in which life communicates with us, and learn to listen.

My Thoughts —

"Nothing happens by itself...it all will come your way, once you understand that you have to make it come your way, by your exertions."

-- Ben Stein

TODAY I WAS attending a conference in Arizona to promote my second book. As I walked around visiting with some of the vendors, I came upon a woman who was selling some merchandise, and her eyes lit up when she saw my badge and that I was from San Antonio, Texas. She asked me if I knew a certain couple, friends of hers in San Antonio, and I told her that I knew the same couple very well. She said that this was an unbelievable coincidence. She had been wanting to send them some merchandise but had not had the time to do so. She asked me if I would take the merchandise back to San Antonio with me and deliver it to the them, and, of course, I said yes. The vendor was beside herself with joy. I was smiling, too, delighted that we had all been touched once again by the hand of synchronicity.

My Thoughts —

"Learn to pause, or nothing worthwhile will catch up to you."

-- Doug King

I WAS CONTINUING on my tour to promote my book, and found myself at another conference. I was wondering why I made the trip – there didn't seem to be much interest in my book, and I was starting to feel I had wasted my time. I went in to listen to a lecture, and I sat down next to an elderly couple. As we struck up a conversation, I began to realize just why I had come to this conference. The gentleman I sat next to was going through some major life transformations, and as I talked to him about my books, he asked if he could purchase them. I gave him both copies, and the next day when I attended another lecture, there, sitting in the room, was the elderly couple, with an empty chair beside them. I sat down with them, and the gentleman told me that, in one night, he had finished one book and was almost finished with the other, and how much my books were helping him. He was thanking me profusely while in my head and heart I was thanking Spirit for giving me the opportunity to be of service to him.

My Thoughts —

"I do the very best I know how — the very best I can; and I mean to keep on doing so until the end."

-- Abraham Lincoln

I HAD BEEN asked by one of clients if I could recommend an expert in handwriting analysis. I said I had known such a person years ago, but I didn't know how to contact her. I promised my client that I would do some research and get back to her, but I wasn't having any luck in finding a way to contact the expert. Then, a couple of days after our conversation, I went to a medical laboratory to get the blood work for my yearly checkup done, and when I entered the waiting room there, waiting as well, was the handwriting expert I'd been trying to locate. She saw my face light up when I saw her, and I told her about my client, her needs, and my efforts to find her. I put the two women in touch with each other, all the time in awe of how life works. Set your intentions and then pay attention. It is amazing how well, and how often, synchronicity works.

My Thoughts —

"Impossible things are happening every day."

-- Author Unknown

My business has been in a low cycle, and during such times I become very cognizant of everything I do, and everything I watch for. I am watchful because I am looking for signs that the rhythm is changing. If I try to force a change in my business during my low rhythms, I've found I am met with much resistance. But I believe a higher power is at work for me during these times, and a recent event in my life confirmed that such a power does indeed work to help me. I was watching television when a commercial came on that was set in an airport. People were holding up signs with names on them as passengers departed from the airplane. One of the signs said "Nelson," which reminded me of an old client of mine that I had not heard from in some time. The very next day I get a call from my client, Mr. Nelson, and he indicated that he had been promoted and wanted to do some training with me. I was smiling over the telephone – partly because I was glad to have the new business, but for other reasons as well!

My Thoughts —

"The difficulty lies not so much in developing new ideas as escaping from old ones."

-- John Maynard Keynes

TODAY I TERMINATED a consulting assignment with a company that I have worked with for the last six years. Although I knew ending our relationship might initially have a negative impact on my finances, it was time for me to move on. On the last day of consulting for this company, one of my clients there told me I should call his wife, who worked for a large school district. I got on the telephone immediately and called, and we met. She decided that they would engage my services, and working with her school district has turned out to be a major training and consulting assignment for me. Not only have I enjoyed working with her and her co-workers, but I was reminded once again of how the hand of synchronicity operates. It is as if "one door opens when another one closes."

My Thoughts —

"Fire is the test of gold; adversity, of strong men."

-- Lucius Annaeus Seneca

As I was driving in my car today, I was thinking about how many of my clients feel that they are working in jobs that no longer inspire them. But though they recognize that they are unhappy, they don't know what they want to do; nor are they willing to risk making a change. I was thinking to myself that I needed to find a resource that I could refer these clients to, one that would help them. I turned on the radio and it was tuned to National Public Radio. The program was about making life changes, and they were interviewing a man name Po Bronson who has written a book entitled *What Should I Do with My Life?* Listening to Mr. Bronson describe the book, I realized it was exactly what I needed as a resource, and I called some my clients right away to tell them about it. I thought about the bible verse that suggests "Ask and you shall receive" as I reflected on this incident.

My Thoughts —

"There is a visible world and another world that is not visible to the eye. It is in this world that a force is at work which wants to work only for our benefit."

-- Author Unknown

As WE WERE reading the paper this evening, my wife and I both noticed that two of our favorite musical groups were coming to San Antonio to perform in concert. Before we could even get on the telephone to order tickets, we received a call from a friend who has a ticket agency here in San Antonio. He had some extra tickets to both concerts and wanted to know if we could use them. Of course, we were elated. I talked with my wife later that evening about the awesome power of synchronicity. Did we attract this call by a deep desire on our part? Were our thoughts so powerful that we instantly manifested what we desired? Or is it just that these kinds of happy events are just chance or good fortune? As an observer of life, one who pays close attention to these "coincidences," I am convinced that there is no such thing as *chance*. What is possible for us? What forces surround us that assist in contributing to synchronistic events?

My Thoughts —

"Today I saw the face of God and I was looking in the mirror."

-- Author Unknown

RECENTLY, THE SAN Antonio Spurs won a basketball game as the result of a "chance" event. Spurs player Steve Kerr took the entire team out to dinner the day before the game. Only the Spurs' starting guard, Tony Parker, was missing, as, for some reason, he elected to stay behind in the hotel room. Instead of eating with the team, Tony ordered room service. His meal gave him a case of food poisoning and he was unable to play in the game the next day. So Steve Kerr played for him - and because of his excellent performance, the Spurs won the game. Although everyone felt bad for Tony Parker, all the television announcers were remarking how fortunate it was to have Steve Kerr stepping in as the substitute. I looked at this story from the viewpoint of another synchronistic event. Would the Spurs have won if Tony Parker played but was not feeling well? In any case, I was happy for the Spurs that they won.

My Thoughts —

*"You make good fortune when you believe
you deserve good fortune."*

-- Chinese Fortune Cookie

CHAPTER THIRTEEN

CREATION

"All serious daring starts from within."

-- Eudora Welty

CREATION

(n. conception, birth, genesis, origination, heaven and earth)

ONCE UPON A time, a farmer had some puppies that he needed to sell. He painted a sign advertising the four puppies, and he nailed it to a post at the edge of his yard. As he was driving the last nail into the post, he felt a tug on his overalls, and he looked down into the eyes of a little boy.

"Mister," the little boy said, "I want to buy one of your puppies."

"Well," said the farmer, as he rubbed the sweat off the back of his neck, "these puppies come from fine parents and cost a great deal of money."

The boy dropped his head for a moment. Then reaching deep into one of his pants pockets, he pulled out a handful of change and held it up to the farmer. "I've got thirty-nine cents. Is that enough to take a look?"

"Sure," said the farmer. And with that he let out a whistle. "Here Dolly!" he called.

Out of the doghouse and down the ramp ran Dolly, followed by four little balls of fur. The little boy pressed his face against the chain link fence. His eyes danced with delight. As the dogs made their way to the fence, the little boy noticed something else stirring inside the doghouse. Slowly another ball appeared, this one noticeably smaller.

Down the ramp it slid. Then in a somewhat awkward manner, the little pup began hobbling toward the others, doing his best to catch up. "I want that one," the little boy said, pointing toward the runt. The farmer knelt down at the boy's side and said, "Son, you won't want that puppy. He will never be able to run and play with you like these other dogs would."

243

With that the little boy stepped back from the fence, reached down, and began rolling up one leg of his trousers. In doing so he revealed a steel brace running down both sides of his legs, attaching itself to a specially made shoe. Looking back up at the farmer, he said, "You see sir, I don't run too well myself, and he will need someone who understands."

With tears in his eyes, the farmer reached down and picked up the littlest pup. Holding it carefully he handed it to the little boy. "How much?" asked the little boy. "No charge," answered the farmer. "There's no charge for love."

--- Story distributed via the internet –
author unknown

"There's no charge for love" still resonates in my heart. This story reflects the essence of creation. At the core of everything in our universe is the power of love. Think about the forces that keep matter together. What force binds the electrons and other particles? Love is the most powerful force in the universe, and we are intimately connected to this force because, at our essence, we are spirit, and spirit is love.

We have been on an amazing journey in this book, and at this point, you have reached a milestone – a point at which you can enjoy the fruits of your labor. I have tried to convey to you my belief in the power of your thoughts, your words, and your actions, and I have asked you to consider that you are a divine being, and that whatever you desire is ready to be brought to you if you follow certain steps. I have also asked you to consider the *source* from which all creation springs.

I have discussed thirteen attributes in this book, and I am asked often by my clients which attribute I consider to be the most important. All of them are important and synergistic – but the attribute I consider to be the most important is the power of focus. It appears to me that by holding in our thoughts the very thing we desire and by seeing the world through the eyes of our divinity, the very thing we desire becomes manifest.

By the power of focus, you are literally birthing a world — your world. What do you want this world to look like? What work do you envision yourself engaging in that will touch the very depths of your heart? Can you envision infinite prosperity in your life? Can you see yourself attracting fulfilling relationships? Is your health vibrant, and are you energetic? Can you see each moment as being filled with enthusiasm, inspiration, and passion?

There is a science to focus, and to the dynamic that impacts creation, based on the thoughts to which we give our attention. Imagine in your mind's eye that in the physical realm, matter goes through many changes depending on the nature of external influences. For example, in a solid piece of matter, molecules show a high degree of regularity. If you were to raise the heat (external influence) on this solid, it would turn into liquid, much the same way an ice cube would if you put a flame under it.

In the liquid state, the molecules are arranged in a new pattern that is constantly shifting and changing. If you applied a higher degree of heat to the liquid, it would turn into vapor, with the molecules arranged into a totally new alignment. And if the heat was raised still higher, then the vapor would turn into a gaseous state. The atoms would continue to rearrange and turn into electrons and eventually into plasma.

The interesting thing to realize in this example is that the plasma and the solid – whatever their pattern - are still part of one another. They are only in a different state. In the human realm, there is a parallel process going on that is at the heart of the power discussed in this book.

In the human realm, you, being a soul, receive an impulse from Source - since all things come from source. That source is in the form of an idea. Using your imagination, you begin raising the heat on your idea. You increase the heat (an external influence) by realizing that your idea is a core desire — something you really, really desire. You create a vision in your mind's eye for your idea and you set your intention to launch your idea.

You then take your idea and you plant it in your heart, raising the heat even further on your desire. You begin to set the conviction for what you desire and you begin to act on your idea in an inspired way. You "feel the feeling."

Now, your intensity is increased by designing the blueprint of your idea. Up to this point, your process has been internal. Now you are starting to link your external world to your idea. You set a goal, and you begin to focus on that goal not only internally, but externally as well. You pay attention as events start occurring that move you towards the manifestation of your idea. You act with enthusiasm, acting as if you know your intention will truly happen. Remember that enthusiasm means to be "enthous," or to be in God. Now the heat is really rising.

Finally, you participate in the outcome as your invisible idea becomes manifest. Your idea becomes solid. It was attracted to you because of the intensity behind your desire. You pay attention to the synchronistic events that lead you to the manifestation of your desire. And then you finally celebrate in the creation – in your external life - of your desire.

The attraction of your desire is in direct proportion to your core desire and your focus. How much do you really want what you desire, and can you keep your focus each day until what you desire manifests?

A gentleman named J.E. Boodin once said that creation is "the shaping of indifferent matter into world of value." I have always said that I believe the world of spirit or God to be impersonal. It is "indifferent". It just *is*. It responds to external influences - and our thoughts and our words *are* external influences. The "world of value" is the quality of our world that is directly related to the quality of our thoughts, words, and actions.

All physical creation originated from a thought. Your life is a reflection of what has come from inside of you. Now you know how to make your hopes, wishes and dreams come true!

ACTION STEP

IN THIS, YOUR last action step, you may feel like I am not asking you to do anything at all. In this step, I am asking you to simply observe your life for a while, until your idea manifests. Once it does manifest, I would like you to journal the series of events that led to the manifestation of your desire. Did you ever lose confidence during the process? Did you, at any time, fear your idea would not happen? How did you get back on track? Were you surprised at "how" your idea manifested? Now that you have manifested an idea, do you want to consider another hope, wish, or dream? Life is awaiting your direction!

AFFIRMATION

I am deeply grateful for the power of creation, and each day I commit to understanding my divinity and creating a world for myself that is filled with love and abundance — a world that I deserve!

OUR LIVES ARE a reflection of our belief patterns. We form our beliefs based on the influences in the environments in which we grew up. We are influenced by our parents, our teachers and our friends. We are affected by what we see on television, what we hear on the radio, and what we read in the newspaper. Unfortunately, we sometimes form belief systems that are not based in truth, and our lives will nonetheless be a reflection of those belief systems. Until we change our limiting beliefs, we will only be creating those beliefs. Creation offers us a multitude of possibilities. Free will allows each of us to decide what we believe and what choices we will make. That is why our lives are a reflection of our belief patterns.

My Thoughts —

"If you sow a thought you reap an act;
If you sow an act you reap a habit;
If you sow a habit you reap a character;
If you sow a character you reap a destiny."

-- Eastern Wisdom

David D. Dameron

Several years ago I started a bookstore, and I was very inspired by this new venture. To save some money, I decided to look for pre-made bookshelves instead of building shelves. I took measurements and determined I needed fourteen bookshelves. I began driving around and going to garage sales, and one day, for no reason I could identify, I felt compelled to drive down a certain street. As I was driving down the street, I noticed something in the yard of a house. Approaching the house, I could see that there were bookshelves sitting in the yard with a "For Sale" sign on them. As I got out of my car, I began counting the shelves in the yard, and there were exactly fourteen. I am amazed at the power of creation and what is possible when I hold my intention in my awareness and believe in possibilities!

My Thoughts —

"Keep score with results."

--Author Unknown

TODAY I CAME to the realization that God is everywhere. When I am setting my goals, I do so literally "within" God. I am beginning to understand that I have a tendency to concentrate too much on the end results. I need to pay closer attention to the "source" of my abundance, which is God. I believe that I have been conditioned to believe that only hard work brings what I desire in life - and I have much evidence to show that hard work does pay off. Yet, I have discovered that I feel I have to make things happen because I do not trust God. I am learning how to surrender and let God work through me, rather than believing, at heart, that I can only make things happen.

My Thoughts —

"None of us suddenly becomes something overnight. The preparations have been in the making for a lifetime."

-- Gail Godwin

How DO I best support my spirit in manifesting my hopes, wishes, and dreams? I do so by holding in my mind's eye the very thing I desire, and by holding the feeling in my heart for the very thing I desire. I pay attention and take actions when I feel guided to do so. Creation is a co-created process. I work with Spirit and Spirit works with me. Whenever I feel stuck or unsure of what to do in my life, my internal guidance asks me four words: "What do you desire?" Holding my desire in my consciousness is similar to watering a dry seed planted in the ground. The seed cannot grow without water. So it is with our ideas – they cannot happen outside of consciousness. I am a divine being and all that I desire is merely a matter of me realizing my divinity and claiming it.

My Thoughts —

"The key to happiness is having dreams; the key to success is making them come true."

-- Author Unknown

YESTERDAY I WITNESSED a miracle at my bookstore. I had been called a few weeks earlier about sponsoring a book signing for the leader of a spiritual group called Eckankar. I agreed and we set up the details of the signing – the date, and time. On the day of the book signing, people started arriving at 3:00 p.m. for a 7:00 p.m. signing. The store was filled with people, and they were lined up in the parking lot. At the end of the night, I made exactly $1,000.00 profit from the book signing, which was, to the dollar, the amount I needed to pay off a bill to one of my book distributors. I am amazed at the power of creation – at the way things happen just as I need them to. Synchronicity and creation are intimately connected with one another. I offer deep gratitude to the Source that allows for this process of creation to occur.

My Thoughts —

"One's destination is never a place, but rather a new way at looking at things."

-- Henry Miller

I WAS THINKING about divine timing today. Why do some things I desire manifest right away while other things take much longer? When it comes to creation, I have learned not to assign time limits when I'm trying to manifest something. I have discovered that there is an intelligence running the universe that is much wiser than my human expectations. The key to divine timing is to remain patient, hold the intention, and remain focused. Then sit back and watch the magic and the synchronistic events that occur, and that bring your desire into physical reality. My challenge is that my physical eyes want to see it right away. But I am learning to see with my spiritual eyes instead.

My Thoughts —

"Every day is a miracle."

-- James Gould Cozzens

WHEN I SAY we live in God, I am referring to the fact that we live in God's consciousness and God lives in our consciousness. This relationship is impersonal in the way it operates. It does not judge, yet it operates according to certain laws. For example, for every cause, there is an effect. Effects and causes happen in consciousness. When intention is infused with consciousness, then manifestation occurs. Think of consciousness as a match waved beneath a piece of paper covered in invisible handwriting. The heat from the match makes the writing appear on the paper. This is how consciousness and physical reality interact. Just as the writing is invisible without the heat, nothing exists outside of consciousness. The quality of creation, then, is directly linked to the quality of consciousness.

My Thoughts —

"That it will never come again is what makes life so sweet."

-- Emily Dickinson

I LEARNED TODAY not to worry about the "hows" of what I desire. I sometimes obsess about "how" things are going to happen. I am learning that I need to concentrate on "what" I want and leave "how" to Spirit. I am in awe of this invisible process which is at work – it is totally subjective. It takes our concentrated thoughts and our heart's desires and goes to work to bring the pieces together to manifest the very thing that we have declared we want. *Nothing* is held back from us, especially if it is a core desire. This is why I keep extensive journals to remind me "how" things in my life actually happened. It is in these journals that I have discovered a wonderful and loving power at work called Spirit. My challenge is to learn how to work with this power and not let my pessimistic thinking get in the way!

My Thoughts —

"If the only prayer you say in your whole
life is 'thank you,' that would suffice."

-- Meister Eckhart

CREATION IS AN inside-out process. Everything happens in consciousness. Whether or not you are paying attention to your thoughts, words and actions, you are still attracting the very thing you are putting out. In order to manifest your hopes, wishes and dreams, you must live the dream. This means not only focusing your attention from the inside out while holding your vision; it also means living your life each day as if what you desire has already happened. Remember that your life is a reflection of your beliefs. Define your core values. Decide what you really want, and then live those core values each day, taking the proper actions to bring your desires into physical reality. We have spent centuries working the process of manifesting things from the outside. It's time to lighten our loads and turn to our spirits within.

My Thoughts —

"We are destined to evolve beyond the nature of duality."

-- Gary Zukav

IT TAKES MORE energy to work on what we want "by the sweat of the brow" than it does to work consciously in partnership with our spirit. When you come to realize that you are a divine being, and when you can embrace the infinite nature of possibility, you will stand in front of the mirror and throw your arms up towards the sky. And you will say one powerful word with all of your heart, and that word is "*yes.*" I say "yes" to all of my desires. I say "yes" to peace on earth. I say "yes" to infinite prosperity and perfect health. I say "yes" to life. And then in that same breath, I look inward, and I say "thank you."

My Thoughts —

"*He can who thinks he can, and he can't who thinks he can't. This is inexorable, indisputable law.*"

-- Orison Swett Marde

APPENDIX

GOAL WORKSHEET

Goal Statement

MY GOAL IS: _____

_____

_____

_____

WHAT OBSTACLES MUST be overcome to reach this goal?

_____

_____

_____

WHAT OTHER ISSUES are involved and need to be
addressed to ensure success?

_____

_____

_____

_____

| Action required | Start Date |
| | End Date |

_____   _____

_____

_____   _____

_____

_____   _____

_____

_____   _____

_____

WHAT WILL BE my payoff for accomplishing this goal?

_____

_____

_____

WHAT WILL BE my next goal once I've accomplished this one?

_____

_____

_____

ABOUT THE COVER

FOR ALL THREE my books, including this one, I have used visionary artist, Arthur Douët, who has designed these wonderful covers. The following is a letter that Arthur wrote me about the symbolism of the cover for this book. I thought the readers would find his artistic insights interesting.

Dear David,

I HAVE COMPLETED the rough sketch of the book cover on newsprint paper. The flower is ever significant of the unfolding from center. One of the most powerful sermons given by Buddha was when he said nothing but presented a rose to his listeners. Jesus told us to consider the lilies of the field in their state of being provided for by the universe.

When I was a child growing up in Jamaica, I remember experiencing a night blooming orchid - a white beauty that had a wonderful aroma. It seemed to be luminous, and this has lingered in my memory. The flower on your cover was not an attempt to draw my childhood encounter in a realistic manner.

Your flower has many meanings. The upper quadrant of the image speaks of drawing on the Light energy from the Source. The lower quadrant signifies manifestation from the focus seen at the centre. The color, yellow, signifies expansion, orange - courage, and green for growth of the "seed" implanted. Violet speaks of the Divine Source and the color white for purity of unconditional love.

Love,
Arthur
douet@arthurdouet.com

AUTHOR'S NOTE

I WOULD LIKE to offer each of you the opportunity to share with me the changes you've experienced as a result of having read my books. It is my goal to make spirituality *practical.* Your story of actual changes in your life can help make the subjects I deal with more accessible and helpful to readers. If you would like share your stories or comments with me, feel free to write me at the address below. I will not use your actual name in your published story unless you request that I do so. Thank you for your support; I look forward to hearing from you, and learning about your own unique journey and experiences.

David D. Dameron
1504 Cedar Drive
Traverse City, Michigan 49684
www.phoenixrisingbookstore.com

ABOUT THE AUTHOR

AUTHOR, TEACHER AND noted lecturer David D. Dameron is the president of Dameron Enterprises, a training and consulting company. He has been a public educator, a successful corporate executive, and since 1990 has trained thousands of individuals in the areas of time and stress management. He is a graduate of Trinity University in San Antonio, Texas with a Bachelor of Arts Degree and a Master's Degree in Teaching. He is happily married and lives in Traverse City, Michigan with two children and two wonderful dogs. For more information about David, you can access his website at:

www.phoenixrisingbookstore.com.

Printed in the United States
103291LV00002B/103-123/P